GARLAND STUDIES ON INDUSTRIAL PRODUCTIVITY

edited by
STUART BRUCHEY
UNIVERSITY OF MAINE

A GARLAND SERIES

BUILDING COMPETITIVENESS

UNITED STATES EXPATRIATE MANAGEMENT
STRATEGIES IN MEXICO

JANE H. STANFORD

GARLAND PUBLISHING, INC.
NEW YORK & LONDON / 1995

Library of Congress Cataloging-in-Publication Data

Stanford, Jane H., 1939–
    Building competitiveness : United States expatriate management
strategies in Mexico / Jane H. Stanford.
        p.   cm. — (Garland studies on industrial productivity)
    Includes bibliographical references and index.
    ISBN 0-8153-1939-8
    1. Management—Mexico.   2. Management—United States.
3. Management—Employee participation—Mexico.   4. Management—
Employee participation—United States.   5. Organizational effectiveness.   I. Title.   II. Series.
HD70.M6S73   1995
658'.00972—dc20   94-35672
                                                              CIP

Printed on acid-free, 250-year-life paper
Manufactured in the United States of America

CONTENTS

TABLES

Table   Page

FIGURES

ix

PREFACE

As international business has flourished, leap-frogging across the world's borders, a call has been made for a greater understanding of those theoretical concepts that drive competitive advantage; e.g., do certain management practices yield the same results in the global arena as they do in a domestic one? The study discussed in this book was in response to this call; the focus, in this instance, was squarely on the issue of the cross-cultural transferability of management theory.

After an initial introduction or summary of the study, the first chapter discusses the study's conceptual framework, defends its significance, and describes its scope.

Chapter two reviews the literature in three primary areas. The first concerns the transferability issue and cultural relativity. The divergent versus convergent stances on this latter topic are reviewed in addition to an in-depth examination of one well-known theory of cultural divergence. The second topical area centers around participative management or "employee involvement," while the third explores the *maquiladora* industry and concludes with a discussion of two major trade pacts (i.e, the North American Free Trade Agreement and the General Agreement on Tariffs and Trade), especially as these pertain to future direct foreign investment opportunities in Mexico.

The third chapter describes the study's methodology, hypothesis and variables, research design, population and sampling method, and test instrument.

Chapter four gives the results of the statistical analyses and explains the findings.

The fifth and last chapter encompasses a summarizing discussion of the study's findings and draws implications from these results.

Finally, recommendations are made. These suggestions are more fully explained through the development of "A Model for Implementing Employee Involvement (EI) in a U.S. Managed Firm in Mexico."

ACKNOWLEDGMENTS

The development of this study, the research involved in collecting the data, and the interpretation of the findings was a long and, often, arduous task, a task that could not have been completed without the help of many friends and supporters.

At the University of North Texas, I would like to thank Al Kvanli, Lynn Johnson, Mike Beyerlein, and, especially, Don Powell and Rose Knotts. Rose, my friend and mentor, spent many long hours evaluating my work and making suggestions for its improvement.

At Texas A&M University-Kingsville, I owe a great deal to those who encouraged me when the task seemed overwhelming and freed my time to meet my deadlines--Robert Kirby, Darvin Hoffman, Bob Nash, Helen McCreight, Linda Lawhon, and Dalton Bigbee. And to those very special individuals who typed and proofread and lent their technical expertise, I will be forever indebted--John Bonno, Sonya Nunez, and my good friend, Barbara Oates.

I also, truly appreciate all of my other good friends who so willingly listened when I needed it the most; a special note of thanks to Sue Beyerlein and Jane LeMaster.

And to my family, who have always been there with their support and encouragement, goes my deepest gratitude--my daughter, Lisa; my son and daughter-in-law, Scott and Christy; my grandchildren, Austin and Spencer; and, most especially, my husband, Rube.

INTRODUCTION

Management strategies that have the potential to capture competitive advantage are essential weapons of contemporary organizations. In the United States, for example, managers are increasingly utilizing employee involvement (EI) practices to reap the benefits of heightened employee motivation, elevated standards of quality, and the augmentation of overall productivity and organizational effectiveness.

Consequently, for those internationally competitive firms using EI as a strategic tactic, it is important that these management practices be implemented with the same success in foreign subsidiaries as they are domestically. However, a number of contemporary management theorists have questioned whether organizations can experience the same positive results in a foreign context as they do in domestic situations.

Social scientists who raise this transferability issue most often cite national cultural disparities between multinational organizations' home and host work forces as the primary reason for failure. Extra baggage that expatriates sometimes bring with them to a host country, such as biased stereotyping and prejudices, have also been cited as underlying causal factors in the failure to successfully implement management practices.

A well-known study conducted by Geert Hofstede (1980a) over two decades ago supports an hypothesis of cross-cultural transference of management practices as one that is problematic. In assessing managerial values among 40 cultures, Hofstede identified four primary factors or value dimensions that varied widely among national culture orientations--power distance, uncertainty avoidance, individualism collectivism, and masculinity femininity.

Pertinent to the study examined in this book, Hofstede's research drew clear-cut distinctions between the United States and Mexico on three of the four dimensions--power distance, uncertainty avoidance, and individualism collectivism. Hofstede hypothesized, for instance, that U.S. workers would perceive small power distances between themselves and their managers in the hierarchial "boss-subordinate" relationship and would typically seek to further reduce the difference. Conversely, however, Hofstede conceptualized Mexican workers as respecting large power distances in the employee-employer association; in this situation, the worker might conceivably work toward maintaining the distance or further enlarging it. An obvious implication that can be drawn from this contrasting U.S.-Mexico value dimension is that U.S. employees would favor a participative style of management over an authoritative one, while the Mexican employee would expect authoritativeness in the workplace.

Similarly, Hofstede conceptualized U.S. workers having low uncertainty avoidance, while Mexico is viewed as being as high in this cultural value dimension. In an organizational context, the effect of this dissimilarity would be that the Mexican employee would typically seek a high level of organizational structuring, the support of written policies and procedures, and few situations in which risk would be encountered (i.e., risk reduction could be in the form of little or no autonomous decision making). U.S. employees, on the other hand, would assumedly prefer fewer levels of management (i.e., a "flatter" organizational structure) and little or no written policies and procedures. Relatively high levels of risk would be tolerated that could include taking on major decision making responsibilities.

In response to the possible threat of the cross-cultural transference of management theory identified by Hofstede and others, the present study was conducted to investigate the cross-border employee involvement practices between United States parent companies doing business in the *maquiladora* industry and their Mexican subsidiaries. The study's research design was a comparative analysis between pairs of managers in companies operating in the *maquiladora* industry; i.e., in each of the companies in the sample, the U.S.-based manager was compared to his or her counterpart expatriated to a Mexico-based assembly plant.

The focus of the analysis was to determine if employee involvement strategies were being implemented by managers within the two different cultural orientations--the United States and Mexico. A substantive hypothesis, developed from the cross-cultural literature, assumed that employee involvement management practices were being implemented among most of the U.S.-based facilities by U.S. managers and U.S. work forces, while the opposite would be true in Mexico--little or no participative practices were anticipated in the Mexico-based facilities in which U.S. expatriates were managing Mexican work forces. Thus, the underlying premise was that cross-border transference of employee involvement management theory was not occurring due to hypothesized disparities between the two cultures.

The control provided by the comparison of United States parent companies and their Mexico subsidiaries--United States home country nationals managing a domestic workforce compared to United States expatriates managing a Mexican workforce--was a very powerful one. If, for example, a parent company utilized a participative (EI) style of management with a domestic work force but did not practice a participative style in their Mexican assembly plants with a host country work force, there were more inferences to be drawn about these two managers employed by the same company than if the two managers had been employed by two different organizations. Thus, the strength of the assumptions that could be made were stronger because of the dependent relationships among the sample.

The research design called for a simple random sample of 500 United States-based parent companies and their 500 Mexico-based assembly plants drawn from the *maquiladora* industry population. In matching returned responses, 40 home nationals managers based in U.S. parent operations were paired with their 40 expatriate counterparts in Mexican *maquiladora* assembly plants.

The majority of these parent companies were clustered in the U.S. along the Mexico border--Texas, California and Arizona; a few companies, however, were located in the northern United States. Most of the Mexican *maquiladora* assembly operations were located close to the U.S. border in Baja California, Chihuahua, and Tamulipas; only a few responded from Mexico's central interior.

To test the hypothesis, an instrument was developed based on Rensis Likert's (1967) *Profile of Organizational Characteristics (POC)* scale. The *POC* measured four categorizations of managerial styles ranging from extremely autocratic to high participative. An informational form was also used that directly queried managers about their use of teamwork in addition to a number of other questions pertaining to EI management strategies.

The primary statistical procedure used to test the data was the Wilcoxon matched-pairs signed ranks test because of the ordinal nature of the data and the dependent samples. Correlation analysis and contingency tables were additional measures.

Results of the one-tailed Wilcoxon showed that in only four of twenty-two instances was the null hypothesis rejected at the $p<.05$ level. For the other response sets there was not sufficient evidence to reject the null hypothesis. Based on these results of the test statistic, it was determined there was no statistically significant differences between the level of participation in U.S. parent companies and their Mexican subsidiaries on the majority of the test questions.

Thus, the findings in this study led to the conclusion that transferability is not an issue in cross-border management practices in the *maquiladora* industry. Furthermore, it was inferred that EI strategies work to decrease power distances, and uncertainty avoidance thus, overriding or ameliorating the cultural barriers theorized by Hofstede and others to exist in Mexico.

In generalizing beyond the parameters of the *maquiladora* industry, the news is good for the the globally competitive organization--management strategies wielded for competitive advantage in domestic arenas can be utilized successfully in foreign subsidiaries.

I

The Study: Conceptual Framework

The competitiveness of United States businesses has been questioned repeatedly during the last few decades. As Japan and the newly industrialized countries of the Pacific Rim have increased their global market and manufacturing shares, and as the balance of United States international trade has tilted in favor of foreign nations, the question has reverberated from one United States industry to another. American manufacturers have been at the center of this controversy and, as a result, have been challenged by consumers to meet higher standards of product quality and service.

In accepting the challenge, astute manufacturers have focused their revitalization efforts internally and have attempted to revamp broad areas of their organization structures, strategies, and processes (Bushnell 1994). One objective of this renewal effort is the creation of an expertise that has been referred to as "manufacturing prowess" (Morrison 1990, 70). This expertise requires numerous factors (e.g., the development of more effective production processes, the enforcement of stringent measures of quality control, the defense of economies of scale, and the utilization of higher capacity, among others).

However, commanding manufacturing prowess alone is not enough to remain competitive in today's global market. In order to be truly competitive in the global arena, an organization must remain innovative and be continuously willing to improve products and processes and to adapt to the further changes that occur (Daft and Lewin 1993; Drucker 1993; Porter 1991). Bartlett and Ghoshal (1987b), too, state that the ability of a company to survive and succeed in today's turbulency depends largely upon its ability to adapt to the demands shaping the current competitive environment. Thus, "organizational flexibility" has become a key determinant of success in the international arena (Dumville 1994; Fombrun and Wally 1992; Hammer and Champy 1993; Schuler, Dowling, and De Cieri 1993; Tichy, et al. 1992).

Fostering this type of adaptability and innovativeness requires a special type of organization structure. Burns and Stalker (1961) first used the term "organic" to characterize it. Rather than centralized decision making, individuals in every part of the organization are encouraged to make critical judgments, to exercise initiative, and to be creative. Therefore, rather than multiple layers of management in an organizational structure made rigid by procedural rules and policies, an organic configuration is relatively flat and flexible. Varying degrees of democracy prevail--rules and policies are replaced by individual decision making throughout the organizational hierarchy. Pucik (1992, 67) reinforces this concept by saying that leading-edge global competitors share one key organizational design characteristic--"their corporate structure is simple and flat, rather than tall and complex." Kahn and Kram (1994), too, refer to a "new" organization form that is transforming the traditional hierarchical bureaucracy.

To preserve its key characteristics of adaptability and innovativeness, the organic structure must have a compatible management style. The manager of the organic structure must encourage continuous and creative adaptation to changing conditions and take special pains to foster, nourish, and support people who are willing to champion new ideas, better services, new products and product applications (Bronson 1994; Gundry, Prather, and Kickul 1994; Thompson and Strickland 1992, 269). Therefore, a management style that is congruent with the decentralized flexibility of the organic design can best be described as one that champions individual endeavors while simultaneously nurturing supportive relationships among organizational members.

The idea of supporting individuals and their organizational relationships has been an inherent component of a participative management style for many years. Likert (1961) used the concept to describe his "linking pin" theory; McGregor (1960), his Theory Y; and Blake and Mouton (1978), a "9-9" leader. The principle was described in recalling the Tavistock studies in London after World War II, the Tannoy factory in Coatbridge, Scotland in later years, and the Volvo plant in Kalmar, Sweden, in more recent times (Maccoby 1981; Wren 1987).

Contemporary theorists have redefined and relabeled the term "supportive relationships" and the concept that the phrase embodies (Crouch and Yetton 1988; Jago 1982; Lawler 1986, 1990; Maccoby 1981; Margulies and Black 1987; Sundstrom, De Meuse, and Futress 1990). However, regardless of its origins or the nomenclature used to describe it--supportive relationships, empowerment, participative management, autonomous work groups, self-managed teams, or employee involvement--the principle is the same. This type of management is currently utilized in all types of businesses to increase workforce performance and to contribute to the overall effectiveness of organizational outcomes, according to Daft and Lewin (1993), Lane and DiStefano (1992), Lawler (1990), Marks, et al. (1986), Norton (1993), and others. Thus, modern employee involvement practices that call for flexibility and self-management are especially useful in organizations that must innovate and adapt because their competitiveness is in jeopardy.

Unfortunately, a possible threat exists in the use of participative management theory in multinational organizations--a transferability issue has been raised by a number of contemporary international management theorists. Adler (1991), Boyacigiller and Adler (1991), and Hofstede (1987), who have been among the most vocal of these theorists, argue that the successful implementation of management theory by an expatriate firm using a foreign workforce is contingent upon the cultural norms and traditions in the host country being accordant with the underlying assumptions of the theory. Thus, a pragmatic consideration is whether an international firm can experience the same positive results in a foreign context when utilizing management theory as it does in a domestic situation because of the difference in the cultural orientations of the workforces. According to the rationale of transferability proponents, it is possible that a management practice, such as employee involvement, would not be transferable across international boundaries if theoretical assumptions and cultural values were incompatible.

Thus, if the transferability argument is a valid one--if management theories that have proven to be instrumental in achieving competitive advantage in one country cannot always be successfully operationalized in a foreign one due to disparities between existing cultural values and theoretical assumptions--then it is a serious issue with far-reaching ramifications.

STATEMENT OF THE PROBLEM

Employee involvement practices are being optimally employed in an increasing number of firms in the United States, especially in manufacturing sectors. The positive outcomes of this approach to managing typically range from increases in motivation and productivity on an individual level to overall increases in the effectiveness of organizational outcomes (Van Fleet 1991). Therefore, the potential of a United States manufacturing company to successfully implement a participative management approach in a foreign subsidiary with a foreign workforce constitutes the primary problem in this study.

Tangent to the main problem is one concerned with the negative effects of non-transferability on trade agreements among nations, especially the North American Free Trade Agreement (NAFTA), a major trade accord recently implemented among the United States, Mexico, and Canada. Prior to the final ratification of NAFTA, many predicted that lucrative opportunities for U.S. direct investment in Mexico would initiate an upward trend in this direction (Bryan and Baz 1993; Bureau of National Affairs 1991; Kleist 1992; Szekely and Vera 1991). As forecast, the pact's implementation on January 1, 1994 officially launched a flow of expanded direct investments from the U.S. to Mexico, a trend that is predicted to substantially increase (Heenan 1993; Hodgetts and Luthans 1994; Hufbauer and

Schott 1993). Thus, if management practices that have been used successfully in the United States to augment competitiveness cannot be fully implemented in Mexico in United States companies' interest, negative consequences may result for both the companies involved and the success of the trade accord.

SIGNIFICANCE OF THE PROBLEM

The significance of this study lies in (a) the relationship between employee involvement practices and organizational outcomes and (b) the implications for United States companies that will establish future operations in Mexico due to the elimination of most direct foreign investment trade barriers.

A positive correlation exists in the participation-productivity relationship (Lane and DiStefano 1992; Lawler 1990; Marks, et al. 1986; Thurow 1992). As participative methods are implemented in a organization, productivity typically rises. One noteworthy example is a General Electric plant that, after changing to employee involvement, witnessed a 250 percent increase in productivity over a five-year period (Van Fleet 1991, 150). This increase was attributed to the creation of a democratic environment that fostered high levels of worker motivation. The findings of a recent international study indicate that United States firms plan to continually increase future participative management practices, especially highly advanced forms of employee involvement such as self-managed teams, to improve quality and competitiveness (Ernst and Young and American Quality Foundation 1991, 30-31).

United States companies pursuing growth strategies in Mexico through either the *maquiladora* industry or through direct foreign investment would seek an organizational design/management style that had the potential to maximize overall effectiveness. Based on the findings of the Ernst and Young and American Quality Foundation study (1991), the choice could feasibly be employee involvement.

SCOPE OF THE STUDY

The scope of this study was limited in three primary directions. First, the broad issue of transferability, as conceptualized by contemporary international management theorists, was only partially addressed in this study (i.e., one particular management theory was examined to determine if it was implemented in a country where cultural values are assumed to be different from those in which the theory has been primarily propagated). The second constraint was a corollary of the first--only two cultures were involved in this study. Third, no attempt was made to build a cause and effect relationship (i.e., the intent of the study was to ascertain only whether a specific management theory could be implemented in a foreign culture and not to delve into the reasons for the success or failure of implementation).

SELECTED THEORY: MODERN EMPLOYEE INVOLVEMENT PRACTICES

The focus of this research, employee involvement, was chosen for several reasons. A primary reason was that employment involvement approaches exemplify contemporary management thought. From a humanistic viewpoint, this approach perceives workers as unique individuals with unlimited capabilities to contribute to a firm. This perspective of employees is pervasive in modern management paradigms, especially in those that call for participative approaches such as employee empowerment, self-managed teams, and cross-functional groups. Conversely, autocratic managers believe that a typical worker holds an inherent aversion to accepting responsibility, is not motivated, and possesses little in the way of personal initiative to contribute to the organization. From this viewpoint, autocratic managers, when confronted with workers, "must coerce, intimidate, manipulate, and closely supervise their employees (Whetton and Cameron 1991, 343). This perspective of workers is represented by McGregor's (1971)

Theory X. The Theory X model does not epitomize a contemporary paragon of worker behavior, as does employee involvement.

A second reason for examining employee involvement is its potential to optimize the human resource potential of an organization (Beardsley 1988: Crouch and Yetton 1988; Goddard 1991; Hackman and Oldham 1980; Kanter, Summers, and Stein 1986; Maccoby 1981; Margulies and Black 1987; Stewart 1991). Because a participative management approach exemplifies contemporary management thought and is a current strategy used to increase individual employees' motivation and to optimize overall organizational effectiveness, this approach is a relevant theory for studying the implementation of management theory.

SELECTED SITUATIONAL CONTEXT: THE *MAQUILADORA* INDUSTRY

The situational context selected to examine employee involvement theory was the *maquiladora* industry dichotomously composed of United States-based manufacturing companies and their Mexico-based subsidiaries. Thus, this study focused on two cultures--the United States and Mexico. The rationale for choosing the *maquiladora* industry was based on two primary factors. In addition to its international character, the first factor for selection hinged on its internal configuration, and the second concerned the North American Free Trade Agreement.

The Maquiladora's Configuration

The *maquiladora*'s dichotomous arrangement of United States-based manufacturing firms, each with assembly plants located in Mexico, offered a unique opportunity to study the implementation of management theory. A common industry practice is to send experienced United States personnel to oversee the general operations of subsidiary assembly plants in Mexico. Consequently, plants on both sides of the United States-Mexico border are managed by United

States citizens; however, these plants are staffed by workforces that are native to their respective countries. Therefore, in studying the implementation of theory, a comparative analysis was made between domestic and expatriate United States managers.

The Maquiladora--An Investment Model

Another important factor in the selection of the *maquiladora* industry for this study concerned the North American Free Trade Agreement. Many speculated that after the passage of the North American Free Trade Agreement, those seeking direct investment opportunities in Mexico would emulate the *maquiladora* model (i.e., United States technology and capital would continue to be combined with an abundant and low-cost Mexican labor supply). Thus, it is important for United States investors and managers who enter Mexico under the terms of the trade accord to know the compatibility of proven management theory, especially theory that has the potential to maximize a firm's competitiveness.

SELECTED PARAMETER FOR STUDY: IMPLEMENTATION OF EMPLOYEE INVOLVEMENT

In this study, no attempt was made to build a cause-and-effect relationship. The research interest was focused on the criterion variable (implementation of employee involvement) rather than on predictor variables (cultural values, biased stereotyping, etc.). According to Kerlinger (1973), it is common in practical or applied research for the basic interest to be more on the criterion (some practical outcome) than on the predictor or predictors of that outcome.

The outcome or criterion variable of interest in this study was the implementation of management theory--whether or not a participative approach being utilized in the United States can be successfully implemented in Mexico. The many implied predictor variables, or factors that could possibly affect the implementation of theory were (a) differences in cultural values between United States managers and Mexican workers and (b) expatriate managers' stereotypical biases toward Mexican workers. It was also possible that expatriate managers lack of skills to effectively implement a highly participative approach (e.g., not knowing how to organize and facilitate team-work) was another factor that could hinder implementation. Too, it was possible that other factors, as yet unidentified through research, could undermine the efforts to implement management theory. Although numerous barriers could feasibly exist, the focus of this study was to determine whether or not modern or highly participative forms of management could be implemented in United States-managed *maquiladora* subsidiaries in Mexico.

THEORETICAL FRAMEWORK

The theoretical framework for this study is built on several branches of the field of management--strategic, international, and organizational behavior and theory. The field of economics is also an important factor in this study's framework.

Strategic Management

Strategic management is usually conceptualized as consisting of three of four primary levels of strategy-making, depending upon whether the firm is diversified. The corporate-level (diversified) or business-level (non-diversified) is concerned with strategies that will guide the entire organization (i.e., all business units or subsidiaries) into the future, serve as a model for planning in lower levels of the organization, and build competitive advantage. These corporate or business strategies typically have great breadth but lack specific, short-range components. More specific plans are formulated at the appropriate level as long-range strategies are directed down through the organization; the respective order of levels is business (if diversified), functional, and lastly, operating. Corporate or business strategies, as well as operating strategies, played key roles in the development of this study.

Corporate or Business Strategies

The strategies of low-cost and differentiation are integral to the concept of competitive advantage in this study. Continuing debates among theorists concern whether these strategies can be pursued simultaneously and whether one provides a greater advantage over the other under certain environmental conditions, such as a globally competitive one.

Thompson and Strickland (1992) contend that striving to be the low-cost producer is an exceptionally competitive approach in price-sensitive markets, especially when there are many producers of similar or commodity-type products. However, a differentiation strategy can also be a powerful approach when consumer preferences are diverse or when a products uniqueness cannot easily be imitated.

According to Porter (1985), a producer chooses one of the strategies in his Three Generic Strategy model--low-cost, differentiation, or focus (low-cost or differentiation). He asserts that trying to be "'all things to all people is a recipe for strategic mediocrity and below-average performance" (Porter 1985, 12, 13), but cautions cost leaders to achieve parity or proximity in the bases of differentiation relative to competitors.

Counter to Porter's stance, Hill (1988, 401) argues that many firms are required to simultaneously pursue low-cost and differentiation strategies--a combination strategy--because in many industries there is no unique low-cost position. Other theorists also contend that generic strategies cannot be stratified exclusively by low-cost or differentiation; that, in fact, any number of combination strategies may exist (Davis 1986; Dess and Davis 1984; Galbraith and Schendel 1983; Hambrick 1983; Miller and Friesen 1978; Robinson and Pearce 1985).

Miller (1988) included other variables in this debate and determined that generic strategies must be matched with complementary environments and structures in order to promote success. He found relationships between differentiation and uncertain environments and between cost leadership and predictable environments. Miller added that these relationships are more likely to be significant in groups of high-performing firms than in groups of poor performers (Miller 1988, 280).

Corresponding with Miller's study, Morrison (1990, 113, 138) found that low-cost did not typify competition in global industries, which are usually assumed to be environmentally uncertain arenas. Furthermore, Morrison found that, within regionally competitive environments, United States-based competitors overwhelmingly emphasized differentiation strategies. This occurred where competitive positioning was predominantly based on quality offerings; producing high-quality goods and services is becoming the focus of United States international competitors (Morrison 1990, 138, 139). (The term regionally is meaningful in Morrison's study, because his findings suggest that the dominant competitive arena for United States-based companies is regional rather than global. Morrison determined that United States companies do not usually view the world as an undifferentiated global marketplace).

In this study, the single factor that was deemed most relevant was that cost control strategies are very important to manufacturers in the *maquiladora* industry. Dornbusch (1991, 74) claims that, due to high labor costs, it is currently impossible for many United States industries to produce goods and be competitive in the global marketplace; foreign industries are far too cost competitive. This is especially true in the United States electronics and automobile industries, where labor costs have stymied competitive ability (Baker, Woodruff, and Weiner 1992). Thus, many United States manufacturers have found off-shore assembly (i.e., the *maquiladora* industry) to be very attractive because it provides a reduction of labor costs (Asheghian and Ebrahimi 1990; Drucker 1990; Special Report 1991). Wu and Longley (1991, 63) suggested that, after the passage of the North American Free Trade Agreement, lowering manufacturing costs and achieving economies of scale would place

United States companies in a better position to compete with Japan and other emerging powers in the Asia-Pacific region.

However, the premise of this study, that controlling costs is of the utmost importance to United States manufacturers, does not exclude the possibility that certain groups of manufacturers will seek differentiation or that a combination approach is the most strategic one. In the electronics industry, for example, companies may pursue a quality differentiation strategy while striving to be cost competitive. Thus, strategic management theory provides a broad basis for building hypotheses concerning competitive advantage strategies in existing *maquiladora* organizations and in future organizations that make direct foreign investments in Mexico.

Operating Strategies

Another area of strategic management theory is that of operating strategies (Schendel and Hofer 1979). Although operating strategies are a smaller part of overall strategic planning, their importance and the role of the plant managers who implement them cannot be minimized. Thompson and Strickland (1992, 39) cite a possible scenario to illustrate this point: "A plant that fails to achieve production volume, unit cost, and quality targets can undercut sales and profit objectives and wreak havoc with the company's strategic efforts." Because of their significance to the operations of the *maquiladoras*, plant managers were used as subjects in this study. Plant managers are responsible for implementing corporate or business-level plans; therefore, plant managers opinions were considered most relevant to this study.

Organizational Behavior

Management style theories fall within the realm of organizational behavior. The management model that is central to this study is a participative one. Contemporary terminology has made autonomous work group, self-managed team, employee involvement, and other similar descriptors synonymous with the term participative management.

Aspects of participative theory, such as the history and evolution of participation and its contribution to modern industries, especially to United States manufacturing industries, form the basis of this study. Included in the history are names such as Mayo, Roethlisberger and the Hawthorne studies in the 1920s and 1930s (Wren 1987); Lewin and Field Theory in the 1940s (Weisbord 1988); the Tavistock studies and the "sociotechnical model" (Wren 1987); a decade later Trist and Bamforth (1951); Likert (1961) and McGregor (1960) after the century midpoint; Blake and Mouton (1978) in the 1970s; Lawler (1986, 1990), Tarrytown (Guest 1979), and Klmar (Maccoby 1981) currently; and others.

Increases in the use of employee involvement and the positive contribution being made in organizations are the subject of much of the current organizational behavior literature (Crouch and Yetton 1988; Dumaine 1993; Goodman, Devades, and Hughson 1988; Lane and DiStefano 1992; Lawler 1986, 1990; Margulies and Black 1987; Van Fleet 1991). The contemporary model of participative management--employee involvement--is distinguished by its respect for the individual worker and its belief that the worker has unlimited capacity to innovate, to be creative, and to engage in critical decision making.

Organizational Theory

Organizational Theory involves the structure of an organization. The terms design and configuration are synonymous, and are often substituted for structure. All three terms connote a physical layering of management hierarchy; thus, a "tall" organization refers to the multiple layers of management typically found in a highly centralized or bureaucratic organization. Bureaucratic structures function best when incremental layers of management can control organizational decision making through formalized rules and policies. This type of structure can be very efficient in a stable environment; because few changes occur, written rules and policies can serve in lieu of spontaneous decision making. Conversely a flat organization is usually characterized by few layers of management, decentralized decision making, and few, if any, formal rules and policies. Because of the absence of rules and policies and the wider distribution of authority, individuals throughout a flat structure must engage in decision making. The degree of individual autonomy in this type of structure is dependent upon management style; however, a flat design can function better in a dynamic environment than can a tall one. Empowered individuals in a flat structure can usually respond instantaneously to the rapid changes that may occur. Therefore, the more that authority is pushed to lower levels, the more flexible and responsive the organization. This type of adaptive organization represents Burns and Stalker's (1961) organic organization.

The Organic Structure

As United States manufacturers are threatened competitively, they are forced to implement a flexible structure such as the one described by Burns and Stalker (1961). The Burns-Stalker organic model, free of rigid, formal relationships (e.g., communication flows freely in all directions) and unburdened by numerous rules and policies is one that can respond best to strategic moves toward change and innovation. Thus, it was deemed as the appropriate model for this study.

The Strategy-Structure Relationship

Alfred Chandler (1962) first conceptualized the strategy-structure relationship in a classic study of seventy large organizations. He determined that the choice of organizational structure made a profound difference in how an organization performs (Thompson and Strickland 1992). Miller suggests that the complex relationship between strategy and structure is, at times, an interdependent one. However, he concludes that the relationship is dependent and strong among successful and innovative firms and seems "to contribute the most to performance in sizeable and innovative firms (Miller 1987, 7) .

Chandler's (1962) hypothesis of the significance of the strategy-structure relationship, supported by Miller's (1987) findings of the relationship being stronger in successful, sizeable, and innovative firms, served as a prototype for this study. Thus, in this study, a linkage was drawn between an organic structure and an employee involvement style of management.

International Management

Because of international management's broad spectrum of interest, the transferability issue falls within this area of management. International management theorists are concerned with the internal and external factors that affect a global organization. The internal factor included in the transferability issue is management theory. The question posed by theorists concerned with transferability is whether transnational enterprises can experience the same positive results in a foreign context when utilizing management theory as they do in a domestic situation. The externality covered by transferability issue is the world's cultures (i.e., the differences among the nations' societal value systems is hypothesized to be the barrier to transferability of theory). Because the focus in this study was on the internal factor--the viability of domestic management theory in a foreign context--the external factor was considered only as one possible predictor variable and not as a major component of this study.

Cultural Assumptions

A number of international management theorists have debated the question of whether management theories are workable under various cultural assumptions (Adler 1983a; Adler and Jelinek 1986; Bhagat and McQuaid 1982; Boyacigiller and Adler 1991; Doktor, Tung, and Von Glinow 1991b; Hofstede 1980a, 1983a, 1983b,

1984a, 1987, 1991; Laurent 1983; Schneider 1988; Schuler, Dowling, and De Cieri 1993; Triandis 1982-1983). In relatively comprehensive studies, England (1975a) and Hofstede (1980a) investigated differences among cultural values. Hofstede (1980a) examined more than forty cultures and identified four value dimensions that varied widely among managers.

Culture and Biased Stereotyping

The commonality among researchers debating the transferability issue is the assumption that cultural value differences are the barrier or predictor variable. Empirical investigations of multinational firms using other variables have not been as prominent in the literature, even though overcoming such obstacles as biased stereotyping are among the major objectives of many expatriate training programs. The Global Leadership Programme, for example, is an executive training course for prospective expatriate managers. The most important lesson in this program involves minimizing the baggage of prejudices and prejudgments that an executive brings to a new job situation" (Wittenbert-Cox 1991, 52).

Other groups and individuals have also attempted to uncover subconscious biases in order to rid themselves of prejudicial or stereotypical behaviors (FIPSE Transculturation Program for Faculty 1990-1992). According to some theorists, personal interactions, as well as flexibility and sincerity, are useful in overcoming stereotyping. After the identification of national stereotypes or images, Ferrari (1972, 31) suggests that increasing the frequencies of contacts between persons of different nations can lead to more realistic mental imaging. Ferrari explained that individuals often allow a closed, cognitive map about the probable behavior of a foreign group to completely define the other group's behavior. Knotts (1989, 32) describes stereotyping as a form of ethnocentricity and suggests that being flexible and sincere will prevent a biased-thought process.

Economic Theory

The economic implications of increasing trade with Mexico through the *maquiladora* industry and the North American Free Trade Agreement called for the inclusion of economic theory in the framework of this study. Mexico and the United States initiated the *maquiladora* industry in 1965 in an effort to maximize each of their comparative trade advantages. Mexico offered its abundant, low-wage labor supply, and the United States provided its capital and technology. United States manufactured component parts are shipped to subsidiaries in Mexico, assembled with Mexican labor, and exported back to the United States for domestic or export sale (only the value-added in assembling is taxed). Originally, only a small percentage of the assembled goods could be sold in Mexico; however, this percentage has been increasing since 1990, and the ceiling will eventually be eliminated under the terms of the North American Free Trade Agreement.

With the elimination of tariff and non-tariff barriers, direct investment in Mexico from the United States is expected to continue to increase as each country continues to exercise its advantage in trade--the United States moving capital and technology to Mexico to manufacture and assemble goods with low-wage labor. These completed goods will then be exported into the global market. Mexico, a labor-intensive country, will reap the benefits of the usage of its labor to import goods that are capital- and technology-intensive. (In many cases, the import-export exchange will occur between United States firms manufacturing in Mexico and Mexican consumers).

The theoretical basis of this advantage-in-trade assumption is the Heckscher-Ohlin model (Asheghian and Ebrahimi 1990, 34). According to this economic theory, each country should export the commodities that use its abundant factor (factor endowment) more intensively, and import goods that use its scarce factor (factor of production) more intensively.

Based on the *maquiladora*-DFI assumption, the Heckscher-Ohlin principle should continue to be exercised under the terms of NAFTA. One international theorist believes that within a few years the United States and Mexican economies will be relatively free of trade obstacles, but the majority of the conditions that favor investment in a *maquiladora*-type arrangement will continue to exist--the low cost of labor, the proximity of the United States, and so forth (Szekely 1991, 31).

An argument that runs counter to the Heckscher-Ohlin model is advanced by Ohmae (1985) and Doz and Prahalad (1988). Ohmae lists three reasons why he believes shifting production to low labor cost countries rarely yields a competitive advantage: (a) cheap labor tends to be poorly trained labor with lower levels of productivity; b) the importance of labor costs in the delivered cost of products is shrinking with technological changes; and (c) as workers become better trained in low-income countries, expectations and wages rise rapidly.

Ohmae's (1985) counter argument was considered as part of the theoretical basis of this study; however, it was concluded that the success of the *maquiladora* industry and the impetus it has provided for a free trade agreement among the United States, Canada, and Mexico are already effective arguments against the first reason (Batres 1991; Masur 1991; Sanderson and Hayes 1990; Wallace 1991). The third reason has also been examined by several international trade theorists who agree that while Mexican wage rates will increase, they will do so gradually. These theorists contend that it may be decades before a complete equalization is reached. They also explain that the corollary of increased wage rates is greater efficiency and productivity in the Mexican economy (Batres 1991; Dornbusch 1991; Mosbacher 1991; Wu and Longley 1991).

SUMMARY OF THE THEORETICAL FRAMEWORK

In summary of the theoretical bases of this study, four branches of management were linked with economic theory to build an interrelated framework for this study. First, strategic management (strategies) were tied to organization behavior (participative management) in order to next connect organizational theory (the organizational structure congruent with management style and strategies). Once these three were aligned, this linkage was related to international management theory (implementation of theory) and, lastly, the almost-completed infrastructure was coupled to economic theory (the *maquiladora* industry and the North American Free Trade Agreement).

II

Review of the Literature

A review of the literature disclosed a number of topics pertinent to this study. These literary offerings are synthesized and grouped into three general subject areas.

The first topic area focuses on the transferability issue. Because a large number of researchers concerned with transferability consider culture to be a primary factor, the divergent versus the convergent stances on cultural diversity are reviewed. Bias and stereotyping are also discussed, even though their role as problematic factors in the transference of management theory has not been as pervasive a theme in the literature as the broad, general topic of cultural relativity. Geert Hofstede's "four dimensions of cultures" theory (1980a, 1980c, 1983a, 1983b, 1987, 1991) is the principal model used to examine major United States-Mexico national cultural similarities and differences believed by many to influence the organizational utilization of employee involvement management strategies; thus, these are significant cultural relativity arguments underpinning this study.

The second topic area centers around participative management theory or "employee involvement." A brief summary of the evolution of participative management practices is reviewed; however, the primary purpose of this historical section is to introduce the contemporary concepts of employee involvement beginning with Rensis Likert's theory (1961). For this study, the initiation of contemporary approaches in the United States is largely attributed to Likert, because his *System 4* style of management was conceived as being a highly participative one exemplified by cooperative "group" work. The four management styles or "systems" that comprise his interval scale, the *Profile of Organizational Characteristics (POC)*, are discussed because they provide the basis of measurement for this study. A review of the role of employee involvement in organizations today concludes this topic area.

The third topic area includes an examination of the *maquiladora* industry and concludes with a discussion of two major trade pacts-- the North American Free Trade Agreement (NAFTA) and the General Agreement on Tariffs and Trade (GATT) and their potential to affect direct foreign investment from the United States to Mexico. This latter relationship between the two major trade pacts and DFI is deemed pertinent to this study due to the implications for U.S. managed Mexican workforces. The literature reviewed in this topic area was gleaned from the popular literature--newspapers and periodicals--and from recent economic writings and U.S. government documents.

TRANSFERABILITY ISSUE

During the past two decades, a growing number of international management theorists have hypothesized that traditional management models are bound by cultural roots to their country of origin and, therefore, cannot be transferred effortlessly and, very often, effectively across international boundaries (Adler 1983a; Adler and Jelinek 1986; Bhagat and McQuaid 1982; Boyacigiller and Adler 1991; Bronson 1994; Butler and Teagarden 1993; Doktor, Tung, and Von Glinow 1991b; Hofstede 1980a, 1983a, 1983b, 1984a, 1987, 1991; Laurent 1983; Schneider 1988; Triandis 1982-1983; Tung 1993).

Shane (1993, 60) says that different societies have different cultural values which result in " . . . persistent differences in human behavior in different countries." He concludes by stating that when people establish organizations, the characteristics of these institutions reflect their cultural values. Hodgetts and Luthans (1994, 59) say that [national] culture can affect the way companies do business; therefore, they continue, "a major challenge of doing business internationally is to adapt effectively to different cultures" (1994, 59). Butler and Teagarden (1993, 479) underscore this statement with their own: "Conflict arising from differences in business practices, standards, values, and norms guiding behavior are inherent in international business." Kim and Mauborgne (1987, 28) believe "the challenge for executives is to transcend the blinders imposed by their home cultures if operations in foreign cultures are to flourish. Adler (1991, ix) explains the transferability issue from her viewpoint by maintaining that "today we no longer have the luxury of reducing international complexity to the simplicity of assumed universality; we no longer have the luxury of assuming that there is one best way to manage." From this stance, she offers a "Cultural Synergy" model for problem solving in a foreign organizational setting (1991, 111). Similar to Adler's theory, Czinkota, Ronkainen, and Moffett (1994, 279) state that ". . . multinational corporations introduce management practices as well as products and services from one country to other cultures, where they are perceived to be new and different." These theorists suggest a model of "Cross-Cultural Behavior" as a possible solution to transferability barriers. Tung (1993) draws an "acculturation process" model.

The disparity issue between national cultures and international organizations is narrowed to more specificity with Hofstede's (1991) statement concerning the management theories in contention.

> Not only organizations are culture bound; theories about organizations are equally culture bound. The professors who wrote the theories are children of a culture: they grew up in families, went to schools, worked for employers. Their experiences represent the material on which their thinking and writing has been based. Scholars are as human and as culturally biased as other mortals (Hofstede 1991, 146).

Cultural Determinism

Theorists who argue that management behaviors are culturally-imbued actions base their reasoning on the philosophy of cultural determinism. Basically, the argument supporting culturally-imbued theory postulates that incongruities can exist between individual cognitions and the underlying assumptions of a theory. These incongruities render the theory inappropriate or not germane within a different cultural context (Adler and Jelinek 1986; Butler and Teagarden 1993; England 1975a; Evans, Sculli, and Yau 1987; Herbig and McCarty 1993; Hodgetts and Luthans 1994; Hofstede 1980, 1984a, 1991; Jaeger 1986; Polley 1988; Ricks, Toyne, and Martinez 1990; Schneider and de Meyer 1991).

Culture has been defined as the beliefs, customs, values, and standards of behavior shared by a particular group of peoples. Hodgetts and Luthans (1994, 59) define culture as acquired or "learned" knowledge that people use to interpret experience and to generate social behavior; this knowledge forms values, creates attitudes, and influences behavior. Vander Zanden (1965, 17) supports a similar definition:

> Culture provides us with designs for living; it gives us guideposts or a kind of map for all of life's activities. It is the socially standardized ways of feeling, thinking, and acting that man acquires as a member of society.

Haslett's (1989, 20) definition of culture includes "shared ways of life, with sharing on both the concrete level (e.g., artifacts) and the cognitive level (e.g., language, symbols)." Hofstede (1991, 4) uses the concept of "mental programming" to discuss cultural assimilation--every person carries within him or herself patterns of thinking, feeling, and potential acting which were learned throughout their lifetime; the sources of one's mental programs lie within the social environments in which one grew up and collected one's life experiences.

Adler (1986, 8) credits anthropologists Kroeber and Kluckhohn with one of the most comprehensive and generally accepted definitions: "Culture consists of patterns, explicit and implicit for behavior . . . Cultural systems may, on the one hand, be considered as products of action, on the other as conditioning elements of future action." Culture can be defined as having one of the following characteristics: 1a) meanings are shared, and (b) behaviors within the group are influenced by its members.

The Cultural Uniqueness of Countries

The assumption that the world's cultures differ from each other and that each possesses inherently unique characteristics is a widely held premise. Haviland (1987) explains his concept of the demarcation among the world's cultures in the following way:

> A group of people from different cultures,
> stranded over a period of time on a desert
> island, might appear to become a society of
> sorts. They would have a common interest--
> survival--and would develop techniques for
> living and working together. Each of the
> members of this group, however, would
> retain his or her own identity and cultural
> background, and the group would
> disintegrate without further ado as soon as
> its members were rescued from the island.
> The group would have been merely an
> aggregate in time and not a cultural entity.
> (Haviland 1987, 27)

Typically underlying this belief in cross-cultural diversity is the argument for cultural determinism (Ricks, Toyne, and Martinez

1990). This philosophy is predicated upon the belief that the values, beliefs, and behaviors of an individual are largely determined by the greater sociocultural environment to which his or her family group belongs. Those embracing the idea of determinism believe that a society passes its values and behavioral patterns from generation to generation. This process whereby culture is transmitted from one generation to the next is called "enculturation" (Haviland 1987, 31).

Convergence versus Divergence of Cultures

The sociological and anthropological stance on cultural diversity and determinism has evoked controversy among social scientists over the veracity of these two theories. However, in the debate over the divergence versus the convergence of cultures, more social science theorists seem to be on the side of divergence.

Divergence of Cultures

Jain (1990, 209) concludes that there exists among nations striking and significant differences of attitude, belief, ritual, motivation, perception, morality, truth, superstition, and an almost endless list of other cultural characteristics. Brislin et al. (1986, 13) suggests that "people typically have difficulties when moving across cultures. Suddenly, and with little warning, behaviors and attitudes that proved necessary for obtaining goals in their own culture are no longer useful." They continue by positing that people are socialized, in their own culture, to accept as proper and good a relatively narrow range of behaviors. Adler (1989, 27) states emphatically that the nature of all the problems encountered by international managers abroad may be perceived as this: ". . . a conflict between the basic values held by two or more groups of people." Hodgetts and Luthans (1994) also underscore the important differences they believe persist among cultures and the effect of these differences on international management. "Culture can affect technology transfer, managerial attitudes, managerial ideology, and even business-government relations" (Hodgetts and Luthans 1994, 60). Schuler, Dowling, and De Cieri (1993, 434) affirm that "the cultural imperative is an encompassing term that can include aspects of the local culture, economy, legal system, religious beliefs and education." Others hold similar views (Ali, Al-Shakhis, and Nataraj 1991; England 1975a; Evans, Sculli, and Yau 1987; Hayes and Allison 1988; Laurent 1983; Lorsch 1987; Rhinesmith 1979; Snodgrass and Szewczak 1991; Stewart 1972; Tannenbaum 1980).

Limited versus Broad Theories of Divergence

Rather than the broad views of cultural diversity previously described, others believe that diversity among cultures is limited to particular factors. For example, several recent theorists have discussed the influence of culture on a society's ability to innovate. Herbig and McCarty (1993) say that certain cultural "shortcomings" can potentially handicap efforts to develop innovative capacity. They cite several scholars who they say have noted culture's influence on innovation--"a number of not yet fully identified cultural psychological social and institutional arrangements must first exist before people will be moved to obtain, create, use and exploit technology to their benefit" (1993, 19). Shane (1993) examines cultural influences on national rates of innovation. Parnell and Kedia (1994) studied the capacity for innovation and developed a conceptual model that identified the relationships between the constructs of national culture and potential firm competitiveness.

Evan (1975) theorizes that time is a factor that can significantly alter culture and its effect. Redding (1980) discusses culture in terms of cognition. Le Vine and Campbell (1972) include aspects of trust and loyalty.

Ameliorating Cross-Cultural Differences

A number of theorists, attempting to resolve the transferability issue, have offered models to reconcile or overcome the national cultural differences they believe exist--Adler's (1991) *Cultural Synergy* and Czinkota, Ronkainen, and Moffett's (1994) *Cross-Cultural Behavior* models are examples.

Kelley, Whatley, and Worthley (1987, 29), speaking from a strongly divergent point of view, state that it is not whether management attitudes are a function of culture, but rather which attitudes correspond with which cultures. Therefore, they conclude, it is crucial to know whether organizational practices can be modified to adapt to the prevailing cultures value structure *without* sacrificing total organizational effectiveness.

A Divergent Theory of Culture: Hofstede's Four Dimensions

A study by Hofstede is recognized as one of the largest organizational-based studies ever conducted (Pugh and Hickson 1989). In researching forty different cultures, Hofstede (1980a) collected more than 116,000 questionnaires from a widespread multinational organization. Hofstede's data, gathered in 1968 and again in 1972, were published in his 1980 book, *Culture's Consequences: International Differences in Work-Related Values.* His massive study continues to be a focal point for additional research (Yeh 1988).

Based on his 1968-1972 study, Hofstede published numerous articles which focus on national culture (1980c, 1983a, 1983b, 1984b, 1985, 1987). In 1991, Hofstede published his second book largely based on his original study--*Cultures and Organizations - Software of the Mind.* In each of these writings, he explains his assessment of managerial values through four primary factors or "dimensions" that varied widely among managers in the forty cultures--power distance, uncertainty avoidance, individualism-collectivism, and masculinity-femininity.

Power Distance

One of these dimensions, power distance is explained by Hofstede (1980) as the distance that employees implicitly place between themselves and their managers in the hierarchical "boss-subordinate" relationship. Hofstede's (1980, 92) findings led to his belief that the maintenance, reduction, or enlargement of this perceived distance is societally (culturally) determined.

This dimension, as well as the other three factors, can be somewhat similar among or between certain cultures, or can vary widely. For example, in the United States, Hofstede found a relatively small power distance (i.e., because persons in the U.S. believe that everyone is comparably equal in status, they perceive a small power distance between themselves and their managers and may seek to reduce the distance). Conversely, in Mexico, Hofstede found a large power distance. In the Mexican culture, an employee tends to routinely obey orders that are passed down from above because of a common belief in inequality--Mexican employees typically perceive a large power distance between themselves and their managers. In this culture, an employee would typically seek to further enlarge the distance in the employee-employer relationship.

Hodgetts and Luthans (1991, 46) quote a member of a high power distance culture as an example:

> What is important for me and my department is not what I do or achieve for the company, but whether the [employer's] favor is bestowed on me ... This I have achieved by saying yes to everything [the employer] says or does ... To contradict him is to look for another job.

Glaser and Knotts (1993) say that in a high power distance culture, titles and deference to authority figures are common and organizations are structured as vertical hierarchies. Leaders expect to be obeyed, in turn, followers expect leaders to provide direction and answers. Thus, they say, in organizations in Mexico, tradition and rules are honored and knowing bureaucracy protocol is crucial.

Davis (1969) explains that Mexican workers often feel personal loyalty to a manager or "boss" but little loyalty to an organization. This emanates, he believes, from the extended family and a strong father image that predominates in Mexican relationships.

Uncertainty-Avoidance

This dimension characterizes the extent to which persons feel threatened by ambiguous situations and create beliefs and institutions to avoid them. According to Hofstede (1980a), individuals, such as those in Mexico, who dislike uncertainty often have a high need for security and a strong belief in experts and their knowledge. On the other hand, individuals in cultures, such as the United States, with low or weak uncertainty avoidance are more willing to accept risks.

Countries with high uncertainty avoidance (Mexico) have a great deal of organizational structuring, more written rules, less risk taking by managers, and less-ambitious employees. The opposite characterizes cultures with low uncertainty avoidance (United States). In these countries, organizations encourage personnel to use their own initiative and to assume responsibility for their actions (Hodgetts and Luthans 1991, 48).

Individualism-Collectivism

Individualism describes the tendency of individuals to look after themselves and their immediate families only. The opposite, collectivism, marks the tendency of individuals to belong to groups or collectives and to look after each other in exchange for loyalty. Hofstede (1980a) measured these cultural aspects on a bipolar continuum with individualism on one end of the continuum and collectivism on the other.

Individuals in the United States, which in high on the individualistic end of the continuum, display an individual propensity to be more concerned with themselves and their immediate families than with other persons or institutions. In organizations, this dimension provides support for the "protestant work ethic" and greater individual initiative (Hodgetts and Luthans, 1994, 51). Promotions are typically made on the basis of merit.

According to Hofstede (1980a), the Mexican culture leans more toward the collectivism end of the continuum. Mexicans tend to have less support for the Protestant work ethic, less individual initiative, and to base promotions on seniority.

Masculinity-Femininity

Ignoring the usual connotation of the word masculinity, Hofstede's (1980a) definition translates to a cultural value that places a high premium on success, money, and possessions. Counter to masculinity is femininity, meaning that the dominant values in society are caring for others and the quality of life. Hofstede postulates that in cultures holding a high masculinity index, large-scale enterprises are favored, economic growth is seen as more important than conservation of the environment, fewer women hold higher-level organizational positions, high job stress exists in the workplace, and industrial conflict is common (Hofstede 1980a, 419). Parnell and Kedia (1994, 15) further suggest that firms in cultures holding a high masculinity index may have greater capacity for human performance for a number of reasons, but one being that employees are financially motivated.

In cultures on the femininity end of the continuum, small-scale enterprises are favored and great importance is placed on environmental conservation, many women hold higher-level organizational positions, less job stress is found in the workplace, and not much industrial conflict exists.

Unlike the previous value dimensions, Mexico and the United States share the masculine end of the continuum. In a score ranking of masculinity index (MAS) values for 50 countries and 3 regions, the United States had a score rank of 15 and a MAS of 62, while Mexico has a similar score rank of 6 and a MAS of 69 (Hofstede 1991, 84).

Future Change in the Four Dimensions

In his 1991 book--*Cultures and Organizations*--Hofstede discussed future changes that could conceivably occur in the four cultural dimensions identified in his earlier research. To summarize briefly his forecasts for these, he foresees that the masculinity-femininity value will become more a function of age in the future, and the trend will be toward more femininity in cultures. For the power distance dimension, Hofstede predicts little or no change in this value. He believes that the historically static picture of national power distance variances is likely to remain as it is for many years. He states: "A worldwide homogenization of mental programs about power and dependence, independence, and interdependence under the influence of a presumed cultural melting-pot process, is still very far away, if it will ever happen" (Hofstede 1991, 47). He believes that these static differences will also remain true for the individualism-collectivism dimension. However, he does say, that if there is to be any convergence between national cultures, it should be on this dimension.

The strong relationship between national wealth and individualism is undeniable, with the arrow of causality directed . . . from wealth to individualism. Countries having achieved fast economic development have experienced a shift towards individualism. Japan is an example: the Japanese press regularly publishes stories of breaches of traditional family solidarity (Hofstede, 1991, 77).

Hofstede (1991) draws a positive correlation between high anxiety levels and high uncertainty avoidance indexes in discussing the future of this fourth and last dimension. Because he believes various world events--wars and regional conflicts, economic crises, religious and political fanaticism--will continue to create new and higher anxiety levels, he foresees little or no reduction in the overall dimension, only fluctuations in societies as events evolve and then subside.

Hofstede's Stance on the Transferability Issue

Hofstede (1983b, 1987) was one of the first researchers to question the transferability of management theory when he contemplated the applicability of Douglas McGregor's (1960) *Theory X and Y* in Southeast Asia. This conceptual comparison was based on his earlier research findings, published in 1980. Earlier, he concluded that the four national value dimensions can affect human thinking, organizations, and institutions in predictable ways (Hofstede 1987, 11). Using these earlier findings as a basis, he conceptually imposed McGregor's American-based theory against the particular four-dimensional value system he described in Southeast Asia and evaluated the theory's appropriateness. Hofstede concluded that the underlying assumptions of *Theory X and Y* were not congruent with the pervasive societal and organizational climate. He stated: "Because of the different culturally determined assumptions, McGregor's Theory X-Theory Y distinction becomes irrelevant in Southeast Asia" (Hofstede 1987, 17).

Convergence of Cultures

A lesser number of theorists believe that although differences may exist among cultures, they are overshadowed by universalities in values, beliefs, and attitudes. The convergence view is held by Boseman and Phatak (1978); Campbell, Bommer, and Yeo (1993); Dian (1994); Furnham, Kirkcaldy, and Lynn (1994); Podsakoff et al. (1986); and Smith et al. (1990).

For example, Dian (1994) acknowledges cultural and value differences, but offers a "tool kit" for cultural awareness intervention that transcends cultural divergence by drawing upon the "universal design from which all cultures draw their uniqueness" (Dian 1994, 29).

Campbell, Bommer, and Yeo (1993) examined perceptions of appropriate leadership style across two cultures. Predictor variables were hypothesized to be leader style, leader gender, organizational setting, and eventual task outcome. Results indicated that the style itself and task outcomes has strong effects on perceptions of leadership style, while gender and setting had no substantive impact.

Furnham, Kirkcaldy, and Lynn (1994) researched national attitudes to competitiveness, money, and work among 12,000 young people from 41 countries on 5 continents. In this study the researchers were less concerned with cultural value dimensions such as those postulated by Hofstede, for example, but, instead, focused their research efforts on "country group differences based on major geographic/continental groupings in economic beliefs and attitudes" (Furnham, Kirkcaldy, and Lynn 1994, 121).

Podsakoff et al. (1986), in what they referred to as a preliminary test, compared three groups: United States citizens working in the United States, Mexican workers in the *maquiladora* industry, and United States workers in the *maquiladora* industry. Their findings suggest that "despite national boundaries, there was a substantial degree of similarity in the way the Mexican and United States employees dimensionalize leader reward and punishment behaviors" (Podsakoff et al. 1986, 132). They also concluded, on a cautious note, that the underlying nature of several of the relationships among the three groups did not appear to be influenced greatly by situational variables, regardless of the cultural setting (Podsakoff et al. 1986, 133).

Boseman and Phatak (1978, 44) used a convenience sample of twenty firms to investigate "the feasibility and transferability of advanced management knowledge to developing countries." They compared the management functions of planning, organizing, directing, staffing, and controlling of United States subsidiaries in

Mexico with similar domestically owned Mexican firms. In order to investigate the directing variable, the researchers queried managers at all levels of the organization about their management styles. They found that an authoritative style predominated in both the United States subsidiaries and the wholly-owned Mexican plants. In this comparison, the researchers found "no statistically significant differences between the way that managers in United States subsidiaries in Mexico and the wholly-owned Mexican firms perform the functions of management" (Boseman and Phatak 1978, 47).

Relationship Between National and Corporate Culture

In discussing the role of culture in organizations (the unobservable phenomenon, [Fiol 1991]), it is useful to differentiate between organizational culture (the culture internal to an organization) and the culture that is inherent to the society-at-large (the culture external to an organization). In contemporary literature, organization culture is often referred to as corporate culture or organization climate, while the societal culture to which an organization belongs is frequently labeled the external environment, or the societal culture. Each of these nomenclatures is intended to distinguish the internal group from the larger, external one. Schein (1986) makes a clear distinction between the two.

Renato Tagiuri (Gray and Starke 1984, 105) defines an organization's culture in the following manner: (a) it is relatively enduring, (b) it is experienced by the firm's members, (c) it is an influential factor in their behavior, and (d) it can be described in terms of the values of a particular set of characteristics (or attributes) of the organization."

The similarity of definitions of corporate culture and national culture is apparent. In fact, this resemblance can be envisioned as a bridge linking the two--when individuals move from a general society to a corporate society, they take the fundamental axioms of their culture with them.

Terpstra and David (1985, 9) maintain that a business's culture is constrained by the broader culture--"the codes of behavior in the organization do not contradict the codes of allowable behavior in the wider culture but rather select from it." Adler reiterates this premise with the following statement:

> Does organization culture erase or at least diminish national culture? Surprisingly, the answer is no: employees and managers do bring their ethnicity to the workplace. . . . Hofstede found striking cultural differences within a single multinational corporation. In his study, national culture explained 50 percent of the differences in employees attitudes and behaviors. National culture explained more of the difference than did professional role, age, gender, or race. (Adler 1986, 46)

Shane (1993), too, believes that organizational behavior reflects societal attitudes. Thus, the literature indicates that the values, beliefs, and practices of an organization are representative of the larger sociocultural background from which a preponderance of its employees are derived.

Max Weber (Conrad 1990, 10) advocated this theory. "He believed that when people entered formal organizations, they brought with them a long history of living within their culture, of learning how to make sense of their surroundings and how to respond to the situations they encountered." Chisholm (1988) agrees that individuals are not born with expectations about what organizational life is like; they develop expectations through communication with other members of their culture. Thus, in the international business arena, cultural differences are often evidenced by disparities in the values, beliefs, and business practices of the expatriate firm and of the host country (Adler 1986; Austin 1990; Garland and Farmer 1986; Hodgetts and Luthans 1991; Jain 1990; Lodge 1987; Phatak 1989; Terpstra and David 1985).

Significance of Cultural Differences to Organizations

Numerous theorists contend that cultural norms and differences constitute relevant factors in organizational contexts (Adler 1983a; Bartlett and Ghoshal 1987b; Kelley and Worthley 1981: Leontiades 1986; Pearce and Roth 1988; Roberts 1977; Tannenbaum 1980; Torbiorn 1985). Triandis (1982-1983, 139) suggests that culture's significance for organizational behavior operates at such a deep level that people are unaware of its influences; it results in unexamined patterns of thought that seem so natural that most theorists of social behavior fail to take them into account. "As a result, many aspects of organizational theories produced in one culture may be inadequate in other cultures." Byars (1991, 9) implies that cultural differences matter because "organizations tend to hire, retain, and promote people who are similar to current employees in important ways." Asheghian and Ebrahimi (1990, 276) emphasize that attitudes toward work and achievement can vary immensely from culture to culture. According to Schneider and De Meyer (1991, 307) "different cultures are likely to interpret and respond to the same strategic issue in different ways." Whipp, Rosenfeld, and Pettigrew (1989, 565) found that cultures significance to a firm helps "to define the way business is conducted." Adler (1986) emphasized the effect of cultural differences on organizational behaviors with the following statement:

> In culturally diverse groups, misperception, misinterpretation, misevaluation, and miscommunication abound. . . . Stress levels increase and employees frequently disagree, implicitly and explicitly, on expectations, the appropriateness of information, and the particular decisions which must be taken. Diversity increases the ambiguity, complexity and inherent confusion in the

groups process. . . . These process losses
diminish productivity [in the firm]. (Adler
1986, 105)

Many other researchers have reiterated this theme of national
culture's relevancy to organizations (Adler 1983a; Atiyyah 1994;
Bartlett and Ghoshal 1987b; Beamish et al. 1991; Kelley and
Worthley 1981; Leontiades 1986; Pearce and Roth 1988; Shane
1993; Tannenbaum 1980; Torbiorn 1985).

Managing Culture

Some theorists suggest that United States employees have a
propensity to ignore cultural differences or to be unaware that they
exist, to the detriment of themselves and their employing
organizations. Conrad (1990) states that organizational newcomers
often experience culture shock--the sudden realization that what was
taken for granted in another culture is not the same in a new one.
This ignorance or unawareness often results in business negotiation
breakdowns. Many contend that it is vitally important to become
knowledgeable about cultural differences that exist (Barnum and
Wolniansky 1989; Schwartz and Saville 1986).

Maddox and Short (1988, 57) warn that "international business
decisions are affected by intense, fundamental cultural differences. .
. . The failure to consider how different societies operate can
undermine a company's success in a foreign country." Hodgetts and
Luthans (1991, 35) add that, "if international managers do not know
something about the cultures of the countries with which they deal,
the results can be quite disastrous."

Consequently, many researchers support the need for increased
knowledge about cultural differences in organizations (Barnum and
Wolniansky 1989; Schwartz and Saville 1986). As pointed out by
Adler (1991, 97), choosing not to see cultural diversity limits our
ability to manage it--that is, to minimize the problems it causes while
maximizing the advantages it allows." Numerous other researchers

echo Adler's theme of managing cultural differences in organizations (Adler 1983a; Barlett and Ghoshal 1987; Kelley and Worthley 1981; Knotts 1989; Leontiades 1986; Pearce and Roth 1988; Roberts 1977; Tannenbaum 1980). Fiol (1991, 203) offers several propositions for managing culture as a competitive resource.

The Effect of Culture on Managerial Attitudes

Van Fleet (1991, 412), in discussing the national culture effect on managerial attitudes, stated: "Cultural perceptions of the proper relationship between boss and subordinate, which show up in such factors as power distance, can have a dramatic effect on leadership styles in various cultures." Massie and Luytjes (1972, 351), in examining United States cultural values, caution that "attitudes and values do affect managerial practices." Anderson (1983), Austin (1990), Daniels and Radebaugh (1989), David (1991), and Wheelen and Hunger (1990) also note that national culture can effect organizational behavior, especially leadership behavior.

Earlier, Webber (1969, 82) remarked: "The diversity of cultural beliefs, habits, and traditions exerts profound influence on managerial relations. What is thought desirable or worthy in life will influence interpersonal relations, especially leadership style." He substantiated this remark by citing a comparative study between United States and Norwegian factory workers by French, Israel, and As (1960, 82), who concluded that "a positive worker' s response to more participative management in the United States is not matched in a different cultural setting."

Similarly, Taoka and Beeman (1991) recognize national culture as an important function of organizational performance and motivation. They maintain that if the cultural values of managers conflict with workers' values, an insurmountable problem may develop. "In such situations, it would be very difficult, for example, to implement a participative management system" (Taoka and Beeman 1991, 295). Bass (1990, 772) cites several researchers who agree that "the values, beliefs, norms, and ideals embedded in a culture affect the leadership behavior, goals, and strategies of organizations."

Asheghian and Ebrahimi (1990, 282) explain that "differences in family structures and in attitudes toward authority in various cultures have led to differences in authority orientations in the workplace." In cultures where respect for higher-ranked persons is stronger, autocratic managerial decision making is generally expected and accepted. Lorsch (1987, 294) adds that "culture affects not only the way managers believe within the organization, but also the decisions they make about the organization's relationships with its environment and its strategy." Hofstede (1984) explains his theory of how culture effects managerial behavior with the following illustration:

> Management is a symbolic activity; that is, managers influence other persons through wielding symbols that have meaning for these persons and motivate them towards the desired actions. An example of such a symbol is a memorandum written by the manager to announce a change in procedure. Its effect depends on a complex set of preprogrammed interpretations by the receivers: whether they can read, whether they understand the language used, and whether they respect the legitimacy of this decision by this manager. (Hofstede 1984, 82)

The significance of culture for managers in multinational firms is the tendency to retain culturally derived behavioral traits regardless of their assigned location. In essence, domestic managers export their learned perceptions and ways of managing to the multinational firm as expatriate managers. Yeh (1988, 114), in a study of American and Japanese firms, found that "they [managers] maintain the traits of their distinct cultural origins even though they have been operating in the same environment for such a long time [i.e., more than ten years in several cases]."

Bias and Stereotyping

A second factor affecting international relationships depicts the bias that many individuals have toward those of other countries or cultures. Bias is often manifested in stereotyping--those predetermined notions of the characteristics or behaviors of another race, cultural group, or social class. Knotts (1989) recognizes stereotyping as a detriment to management outcomes.

In studying managerial attitudes across several countries, Haire, Ghiselli, and Porter (1966) found that managers expressed little confidence in subordinates' capacities for responsibility, initiative, and leadership. Ferrari (1972, 31) equates this lack of confidence to closedness, or being close-minded. He contends that a national stereotype is closedness in that when individuals exhibit this stereotypical behavior, they allow it to define the foreigner's behavior.

Conclusion of Transferability Issue

The literature supports a theme of culturally imbued actions and behaviors of multinational managers. Of particular interest to management theorists is the study of dissimilarities between domestic and multinational firms; however, the focus of this interest has shifted toward the issue of transferability.

EMPLOYEE INVOLVEMENT THEORY

Edward Lawler, a contemporary academician and management consultant, identifies high-involvement or team-based management as the most successful management style being utilized in organizations. In a recent article (1990), he comments that only two decades ago, a few United States companies began building a new type of manufacturing facility--one that emphasized a high level of employee involvement. Today, he adds, a revolution has occurred as more companies have implemented this form of management. These new plants are noted for the degree to which the workplace is egalitarian. Employees are challenged to control their span of job activities and to direct the way in which work is performed. The typical vehicle for this employee involvement is self-managed teams, where decision-making responsibility is pushed to the lower levels of the hierarchy.

George et al. (1990), Kanter (1983), and Pearce and Ravlin (1987) cite numerous other situations in which application of work teams in industry continue to increase. Pasmore et al. (1982, 148) concluded that the introduction of "autonomous work groups was the most common intervention in 134 experiments in manufacturing firms." Margulies and Black (1987, 385) point out that "participative management, both in terms of specific techniques and as a broad value, has become more utilized in recent years." Beardsley (1988, 138) more emphatically states that, "The most dramatic social and economic change since the Industrial Revolution is the evolution of participative management in United States business culture."

United States industry was slower to accept participative approaches than were management theorists (Collins, Ross, and Ross 1989). Krishnan found that a majority of the 1,400 United States business executives taking part in a 1974 survey of large manufacturing organizations discouraged employee participation in organizational decision making. Apparently, only a few, progressive firms realized that participative management were valuable in increasing quality motivation, efficiency, etc. (Glaser and Knotts 1993). However, seventeen years later, a similar Ernst and Young and the American Quality Foundation study showed a marked difference. The results of their international study indicated that when it comes to organizing 75 percent or more of employees into quality-related teams, more than a third of United States businesses plan to do so over the next three years" (Ernst and Young and the American Quality Foundation 1991, 31). Kanter, Summers, and Stein's (1986, 30) findings support the Ernst and Young study: "a recent survey showed that organizations of all sizes have adopted alternatives identified as participative management, employee involvement, workplace democracy, and quality of working life."

Organizations frequently cite positive results as a reason for increased use of participative forms of management. Positive results are manifested in the form of more satisfied, motivated, and productive employees, which enable firms to be more effective and, thus, more competitive. Bronson (1994) says his consulting firm organizes and facilitates employee involvement teams as a cross-cultural intervention tool--"The teams are created to change or improve existing processes" (Bronson 1994, 61).

A contemporary attitude toward the role of participative management is reflected by the following statement: Organizations that are experiencing success in today's marketplace are moving toward a democratic management process (Levy 1991, 86). Success stories involving employee involvement are not new, however. Beyerlein (Guess 1991, 3) pointed out that companies began covertly using work teams because they provided a competitive edge as long as twenty years ago. As more companies become aware of employee involvement as a competitive strategy, work teams are spreading from coast to coast.

Miller and Monges (1986) meta-analysis supports the current belief that participation has a positive effect on both satisfaction and productivity. An American Management Association survey of 7,200 business managers revealed that managers should adopt a more participative management style (Goddard 1991, 14). Sashkin (1986) avows that participative management is an ethical imperative. Numerous practitioners have lauded the effects of participation on organizational outcomes (Note: Dumaine 1990, 1993; Kusy, Isaacson, and Podalan 1994; Lewis 1991; Magnet 1992; Nulty 1990; Rose 1990; Stewart 1991, 1992; Van 1992; Wartzman 1992). Thurow (1992) says that participatory management raises productivity. Kanin-Lovers (1990) theorizes that one of the most vital factors in organizational successfulness is increased use of participative management.

A significant component of the United States quality movement supports employee involvement. An American, W. Edwards Deming, (1982, 1987) is credited with taking the participative team concept to the Japanese after World War II. He helped to revitalize Japanese industry with employee involvement and his statistical quality control methods.

The Evolution of Participative Management

Simultaneous to a comparable European movement, the United States underwent a management revolution in the early part of the twentieth century; the human relations movement began in the 1930s (Gray and Starke 1984). The initiation of this movement in the United States is often credited to the Mayo-Roethlisberger studies conducted at the Hawthorne Plant of the Western Electric Company between 1924 and 1927. According to Weisbord (1988), Kurt Lewin's 1940s work in field theory provided one of the conceptual bases for what was to become known as participative management. Lewin's 1940s model sought to preserve democratic values, build commitment to act, and motivate learning (Weisbord 1988, 8).

A decade later, the London Tavistock Institute conducted a series of well-known studies. One study that was particularly important to the evolution of participatory management examined productivity changes associated with the implementation of a coal mine assembly line. Management failed to recognize the social importance that miners attached to working in small, autonomous groups; however, the sociotechnical model that ensued from these studies led to increased use of participative management (Cummings 1989; Trist and Bamforth 1951, 3-38).

In the mid-1950s, the participative-humanistic model began to evolve more fully as theorists, such as Argyris (1957), Blake and Mouton (1964), Davis (1957), Herzberg, Mausner and Snyderman (1959), Likert (1961, 1967), Maslow (1965) and McGregory (1960) contributed their ideas. In the 1970s, General Motors' Tarrytown plant and the initiation of an employee involvement process referred to as "quality of work life contributed new dimensions to the model" (Guest 1979). In reflecting on management's evolutionary trends, Wren (1987, 379) equated the importance of quality of work life to the Hawthorne experiments of the 1930s. At the same time, new theories, such as goal setting and job enrichment, began to broaden the human relations model. Simultaneously, contingency leadership approaches began to surface. Stoner and Freeman (1992) credited Fiedler (1967), Hersey and Blanchard (1969), House (1971) and Vroom-Yetton (1973) as major contributors to this movement.

The contingency or situational model overshadowed the participative model during this period because it suggested that other types of management styles could be equally effective. As the 1980s witnessed increased global competitiveness and massive organizational restructuring, however, the participation model once again returned to the forefront of management thought.

Rensis Likert

Likert (1961, 1967), perhaps more than any other researcher, advanced the concepts of modern participative approaches. In defining participative management, Likert (1961, 289) purposed the idea of supportive relationships, and described a management system based on these types of relationships as a "group form of organization." He demonstrated this concept through a "linking pin" configuration. His affirmations of participative management were that "the supervisors and managers in American industry and government who are achieving the highest productivity, lowest costs, least turnover and absence, and the highest levels of employee motivation and satisfaction display, on the average, are using a different pattern of leadership from those managers who are achieving less impressive results" (Likert 1961, 97) .

Likert (1961, 1967) challenged participative managers to develop subordinates into loyal teams. Likert depicted the participative manager as follows: "He is supportive, friendly, and helpful. . . . He shows confidence in the integrity, ability and motivations of subordinates. . . . He has high expectations for subordinates' levels of performance. . . . He coaches and assists employees" (Likert 1961, 284).

Likert (1961, 1967) contrasted participative to authoritative management behavior. In comparing managerial attributes, Likert described the participative manager as supportive rather than hostile, kind but firm, never threatening, and as exhibiting confidence rather than suspicion and distrust.

In Likert's management model (1967), two levels of participation and two levels of authoritative-type management styles are identified. *System 1*, the most authoritative, is called exploitative authoritative. *System 2*, the least authoritative, is labeled benevolent authoritative. *System 3* and *4* denote the levels of participation. *System 3* is the least participative and signifies a consultative participative style, while *System 4*, the most highly participative, represents a group or team approach.

In an instrument developed in the 1960s, *The Profile of Organizational Characteristics* (*POC*), Likert equated *Systems 3* and *4* with numerous employee involvement concepts. Democracy, support, and confidence in the employer-employee relationship are among the underlying constructs in the instrument questions measuring participative styles of management (*Systems 3* and *4*). For example, several questions query respondents about the amount of group work present, and whether decision making systems encourage employee participation. This equation reflects the contemporary version of employee involvement.

The Present State of Participation in the United States

Lawler (1986, ix) asserts that participative theory exists in many forms--employee involvement, quality circles, job enrichment, work teams, quality-of-life programs, attitude surveys, gainsharing, and new-design plants. Each of these forms supports the premise that individual employees contribute substantial value to the firm, that trust and respect exist in the employer-employee relationship, and that decision making should be shared (i.e., the capability for self-direction and self-control are inherent in every human being). Beyerlein (Guest 1991, 3) explains that, "at its best, a self-managed work team gives individual workers more responsibility and more freedom . . . [than other forms of participative management] while changing the manager's role from controller to facilitator."

Employee Involvement Theory Paradigm Shift

Participative management has experienced more than a name change. This paradigm shift from Likert (1961, 1967) to Lawler (1986) has involved emphasis on the structure of the organization and the decision-making hierarchy. Both Lawler (1990) and Kanter, Summers, and Stein (1986) discuss this shift to bottom-up management which began two decades ago. One of the most striking features of the new participative [manufacturing] plants is their structure." They are characterized by very flat structures and extremely wide spans of control" (Lawler 1990, 5). Kanter, Summers, and Stein (1986) recognize that numerous types and sizes of organizations are adopting participative forms of management. They predict an escalation in this trend. Others support the premise that employee involvement is the key to present and future success.

THE *MAQUILADORA* INDUSTRY AND MAJOR TRADE ACCORDS

The number of organizations conducting business internationally is increasing exponentially. Collectively, multinational corporations account for more than 40 percent of the world's manufacturing output and almost a quarter of the world's trade (Bartlett and Ghoshal 1992, 5). This growth has influenced the world economy as a whole and the individual, national economies from which globally competitive businesses have sprung. Between 1950 and 1980, United States firms' direct foreign investment increased from $11.8 billion to $200 billion (Bartlett and Ghoshal 1992, 7). In the 1970s, attention shifted to developing countries, such as Mexico. In these countries, the United States' share of direct foreign investment grew from 18 percent in 1974 to 25 percent in 1980 (Bartlett and Ghoshal 1992, 7). During the past five years, U.S. companies have invested $11.6 billion South of the border and with still "freer boundaries" this figure will increase (Heenan 1993, 6).

One major form of direct foreign investment is the *maquiladora* industry. One proponent of the *maquiladora* industry recently observed:

> Today along the Texas-Mexico border, we can certainly say we are in the best of times as we see the boom created as a direct result of growing trade relations with Mexico. It is estimated, for example, that the trade agreement known as the *maquiladoras* program" is now contributing $196 million per year to the Laredo economy alone in wages, taxes, lease payments, business visitors, purchases of goods and services, retail sales and home sales. (Schwebel 1991, 1)

The *maquiladora* program, a free trade zone, has primarily benefited the Mexico-border regions of Texas, New Mexico, Arizona, and California. This reciprocal program between the United States and Mexico, lifts three trade restrictions: (a) the type of industry that can be established in Mexico (i.e., the assembly of manufactured component parts), (b) the amount of this industry's investment in Mexico (i.e., even prior to the passage of the North American Free Trade Agreement, it was possible for a licensed *maquiladora* firm to have 100% foreign ownership of plant facilities in Mexico), and (c) the amount of assembled goods that can be sold in Mexico (in years prior to NAFTA, the largest percentage of finished goods were exported back to the United States; however, this restriction is being lifted with the phasing out of all tariff and non-tariff barriers among the U.S., Mexico, and Canada). U.S. Commerce Secretary Brown recently stated that U.S. exports to Mexico are at record levels, rising 17 percent for the first six months of 1994 compared to the same period one year ago; e.g., some $24.5 billion in U.S. goods were shipped to Mexico (Mithelstodt 1994, A15).

Thus, component parts are manufactured in the United States, shipped to Mexico where an import bond is placed on them, assembled in Mexican plants, and then exported as finished goods back to the United States. Except for a tariff on the value-added in Mexico, the process is duty-free.

When the North American Free Trade Agreement (NAFTA) was finalized, nearly all trade restrictions between the United States and Mexico will be lifted over a 15-year period. This major trade pact will permit direct foreign investors to experience the advantages that have been exclusive to *maquiladoras* in the past. The accord will open most avenues of trade between the two countries thus, promote the free flow of duty-free imports and exports statistics show that, "on the average, each Mexican imports $380 of U.S. merchandise annually" (Hufbauer and Schott 1993, 19). Too, the provisions of NAFTA will "accord national treatment to NAFTA investors" (Hufbauer and Schott 1993,3). Canada, a United States free-trade partner since 1989, will also reap benefits from this pact.

The expected long-range results of the North American Free Trade Agreement will be the unimpeded conduct of business among the three countries. This free-trade accord, when it was implemented on January 1, 1994, created a market of 362 million people, the largest liberalized economy in the world (Kootnikoff 1991, 5). The long-range goal for the North American Free Trade Agreement is to include countries south of Mexico. Such a North-to-South hemispheric trade alliance would outrival most of the major trading blocs in the world today. The General Agreement on Tariffs and Trade (GATT) is a second major trade accord that has the potential to positively impact trade and direct foreign investment opportunities between the U.S. and Mexico and among other trading partners. If ratified by all involved, the historic GATT can play a major role in the global economy by lowering tariffs and non-tariff barriers; thus, facilitating trade among the 123 countries signing the Uruguay Round on Dec. 15, 1993.

History of the Maquiladora Industry

The *maquiladora* program was instituted between the United States and Mexico in 1965 as a method of easing Mexico's unemployment problem. Under-employment and nonemployment had become especially severe along Mexico's United States border after the collapse of the Bracero Program. That program had previously allowed 500,000 Mexican workers to enter the United States for seasonal agricultural work (Mexico 1989). In order to cope with this surplus labor force, the *maquiladora* program invited labor intensive manufacturing businesses into Mexico. The goal was to place the most labor intensive manufacturing process--the assembling of component parts--in Mexico; hence, the term *maquiladora*, which refers to an assembly plant (Mexico Chamber of Commerce 1990). The capital- and technology-intensive manufacturing processes were to remain in the United States. As a consequence of the dual locations, the *maquiladoras* are frequently referred to as twin plants.

The *maquiladora* program quickly developed into a full-fledged industry. Although parent companies are located as far away as Illinois, Michigan, and New York, the most active participation is along the United States border regions of Texas, New Mexico, Arizona, and California. It is estimated that 95 percent of the foreign *maquiladora* business going into Mexico is United States owned (Mexico Chamber of Commerce 1990).

Bonds on Imports to Mexico

The Mexican government granted free trade privileges to manufacturing companies obtaining *maquiladora* permits. However, a restriction required that a bond be paid on imported component parts as a guarantee that a finished product would be subsequently exported. Hence, the *maquiladora* plants also became known as in-bond assembly plants (Mexico Chamber of Commerce 1990).

Value Added to Exports

A restriction required that a duty be paid on the value-added when assembled goods were exported. Value-added translated into any additions during the assembly process. A licensed United States custom broker recently explained that value-added can include electricity or rent, but most typically is labor. He gave an example of how labor can be value-added. If a partially assembled shirt comes into Mexico containing a completed buttonhole, when the shirt leaves Mexico no value is added for the buttonhole. Other labor costs that arose in Mexico--sewing the sleeves to the bodice, hemming, etc.--are taxed (Corrigan 1991).

Facility Locations for Maquiladora Plants

Businesses establishing *maquiladora* operations have typically clustered near the border to defray the costs of transporting component parts from the United States to Mexican assembly plants. Although a few companies have established assembly plants further into Mexico in recent years. This propensity to stay near the border is typical of most *maquiladora* plants.

The Maquiladora Population

As of June 1994, there were 2,032 *maquiladora* plants employing approximately 468,086 workers (Nibbe and Nibbe 1994, 41). The areas evidencing the greatest growth of *maquiladora* plants have been the proximal cities of Matamoros-Brownsville, Nuevo Laredo-Laredo, and Cd. Juarez-El Paso in Texas, Nogales-Nogales in Arizona, and Mexicali-Calexico and Tijuana-San Diego in

California. As of June 1994, Tijuana-San Diego topped the list in number of plants with 513; Cd. Juarez-El Paso was second with 274.

Types of Manufacturing Plants

Although approximately eleven types of manufacturing industry segments can be found among the *maquiladoras*, the largest sector is electric and electronic goods. Furniture and other wood and metal products make up the second largest sector, "other" or miscellaneous manufacturing is the third, and clothing and other textiles is the fourth. Electronic and electrical equipment and appliances and articles make up the fifth largest segment (Mexico 1989, 16).

Ownership Arrangements

Three ownership arrangements are found in the *maquiladora* assembly plants: (a) wholly-owned foreign subsidiaries, subject to Mexican law; (b) subcontracted ventures, in which the manufacturing process is subcontracted to an existing assembly plant and the client is responsible for supplying the contractor with the necessary raw materials and other inputs; and (c) shelter operations, whereby Mexican-owned and managed plants offer component part assembly to foreign clients under a series of very specific agreements. The first type, wholly-owned subsidiaries account for approximately 89 percent of all *maquiladora* businesses. The last two, together, account for the remaining 11 percent (Mexico Chamber of Commerce 1990, 1-5).

Management-Labor Division in the Maquiladora Industry

One important aspect in the study of transferability is the dichotomous arrangement between United States management and Mexican workforces in the assembly plants. Management's ranks are composed largely of United States citizenry (i.e., parent companies in the United States typically employ United States expatriate managers in the Mexican assembly plants).

The Mexican government advocates a strong management team consisting of employees from the parent company's home country and Mexican nationals (Mexico Chamber of Commerce 1990, ix-9). Because Mexico now graduates more engineers per capita than the United States (Schewebel 1991), it is possible to recruit Mexican professionals for management teams. At present, however, top management positions are dominated by United States expatriates, who often commute to the Mexican plants. The length of managers' foreign assignments in Mexico varies, but a typical assignment is from three to five years (Sherwood 1991). Staff and labor, on the other hand, are composed almost entirely of Mexican-born individuals.

Mexico's Labor Pool

Out of Mexico's 82 million population, 2,576,775 are actively employed in industry (*Mexico 2000* 1990, 51). Of the 2.5 million manufacturing workers, more than 500,000 work in *maquiladora* assembly plants ("Special Report: United States Companies Doing Business in Mexico" 1991).

Economic Impact of the Maquiladora Industry

Due to the rapid growth of the *maquiladora* industry, the economies of the two primary countries involved--Mexico and the United States--have been significantly affected. According to the reports of Mexican officials, "the industry annually generates in excess of $12.4 billion in products and over $3 billion of value-added income for Mexico." It ranks second only to Mexico's petroleum industry as a generator of foreign exchange (Mexico 1989, 2-3).

The North American Free Trade Agreement
and the Maquiladora Industry

Many have suggested that the *maquiladora* industry provided
the impetus for the free trade pact among Mexico, the United States,
and Canada--NAFTA (Sanderson and Hayes 1990; Szekely 1991).
This opinion was supported in an early North American Free Trade
Agreement negotiation meeting:

> The *maquiladora* program has been the
> pathfinder to bulldozing commercial
> roadblocks between our two countries
> [United States and Mexico]. Today it is the
> most successful Mexican-American program
> of any kind ever undertaken, and a godsend
> to the working class in the northern part of
> Mexico. (Cypher 1991, A19)

Even though they had to convince skeptics in both countries,
Presidents George Bush and Carlos Salinas de Gortari met and
jointly concurred that a free trade pact would "create jobs and provide
opportunities for citizens in both . . . countries" (Kootnikoff 1991, 8).
As a true bilateral trade agreement, it surpasses the restricted terms
of the *maquiladora* program and offers employment incentives,
direct foreign investment opportunities, and an increase in the overall
economies of the countries involved. This estimated augmentation of
the U.S. economy was supported recently with a statement by U.S.
commerce Secretary Ron Brown: "the North American Free Trade
Agreement is proving to be a boom to the economies of the United
States, Mexico, and Canada" (Mittelstadt 1994, A15).

Job Opportunities

According to Ambassador Negroponte, for every additional
billion dollars the United States exports, 25,000 jobs are created. In

1990 alone we exported $30 billion worth of products to Mexico (Negroponte 1991, 9). Others believe that the North American Free Trade Agreement will continue to create more jobs on both sides of the border (Dornbusch 1991). Batres (1991, 90) reports that a study conducted by the United States International Trade Commission in 1988 revealed that between 1980 and 1985, the number of United States jobs resulting from the manufacture of components shipped to Mexico for assembly increased from 230,000 to 500,000, a 17 percent annual rate of growth.

Increased Level of Training and Wage Rates

Mexican workers are expected to benefit from the pact because levels of training, wages, and standards of living are expected to increase. Batres (1991) and Szekely and Vera (1991) cite the experiences of international companies and workers in Eastern Asia to confirm this point.

Direct Foreign Investment (DFI)

Direct United States investments in Mexico made possible through the *maquiladora* industry and now on a much greater scale, through NAFTA, will provide United States manufacturers with a competitive advantage in global markets (Batres 1991; Dornbusch 1991; Szekely 1991). Masur (1991, 101) cites testimonials from two major auto parts manufacturers, the maker of ceramic magnets, a repairer of cordless telephones, and an assembler of electric harnesses in support of this statement. Kleist (1992), too, says that Mexican companies have become an increasing popular place for Americans to invest their money--"of the $9.9 billion in direct foreign investment that poured into Mexico last year, nearly one-third of it came through American Depository Receipts (Kleist 1992, C8).

III

Methodology

The methodology used in this study is described in this chapter. Included in the methodology are a discussion of the sample, the hypothesis and variables, the research design, testing instrument, collection procedures, and the procedures used for treatment and interpretation of the data.

HYPOTHESES AND VARIABLES
SUBSTANTIVE HYPOTHESIS

A review of the literature revealed a problem in the transfer of management theory across international borders. From this synthesis, a hypothesis was formulated. This substantive hypothesis states that employee involvement practices, especially advanced forms that call for teamwork, are not being implemented in the Mexican subsidiaries of United States parent companies. Thus, in this comparative analysis between United States-based parent companies and their Mexico-based *maquiladora* subsidiaries, it was assumed that United States plants were practicing higher levels of participation than were Mexico plants.

The implicit argument underlying this hypothesis is that the Mexican culture or the stereotypical biases of United States expatriate managers generally serve as a barrier to the implementation of employee involvement practices. The criterion variable of implementation of management theory was studied for the effect of the predictor variables, cultural value differences or managerial stereotyping. The surrogate for the criterion variable was the presence or absence of employee involvement practices in the *maquiladora* industry. The supposition of lower levels of participation in the Mexico *maquiladora* assembly plants--thus, the non-implementation of theory--was tested through a null hypothesis.

Rationale of Substantive Hypothesis

The substantive hypothesis in this research problem was that highly participative forms of management comparable to Likert's *System 4* or an employee involvement approach were not being implemented in the *maquiladora's* Mexican assembly plants. The implicit argument in this hypothesis was that the cultural value system of the Mexican nation acts as a barrier to the application of an advanced employee involvement, team-based approach and that United States expatriate managers have predetermined, largely unfavorable concepts of the behavior of Mexican workers. These predetermined cognitions often exhibit themselves through mental biases or stereotypes.

Tested Hypothesis: Null and Alternate

To test the substantive hypothesis, it was translated into operational and experimental terms (Kerlinger 1973). Statistical testing was used to determine whether this hypothesis was rejected or failed to be rejected.

H_o: The level of employee involvement in a United States parent company is less than or equal to that of a Mexican *maquiladora* subsidiary.

H_a: The level of employee involvement in a United States parent company is more than in a Mexican *maquiladora* subsidiary.

Predictor and Criterion Variables

This study focused on the criterion variable of implementation of management theory. In other words, the real interest in this research was whether participative management practices, especially those incorporating high levels of employee involvement, are being implemented in the Mexico-based subsidiaries of United States parent companies that comprise the *maquiladora* industry.

Surrogates for the Criterion Variable

In order to be able to test the criterion variable, surrogates or testable representatives of this variable were determined. In this case, the surrogates were the presence or absence of employee involvement practices in the *maquiladora* industry and, if present, the level to which they were present.

Thus, on a scale ranging from one to twenty, the measuring instrument determined initially if participative management practices or non-participative practices (authoritative ones) were being used in both United States and Mexico plants. On the scale, these styles are represented by questions that correspond to Likert's *System 1* (exploitative authoritative), *System 2* (benevolent authoritative), *System 3* (consultative participative) and *System 4* (participative group) styles of management. If an employee involvement style was being utilized by the manager in a plant (United States or Mexican), then the test instrument measured the degree of participation, ranging from a low level of involvement (*System 3*) to the highest level (*System 4*). Through this measurement, a comparison was made between the particular United States plant manager and his or her counterpart in Mexico (See Table 1).

Table 1.--Relationships among Variables, Surrogates, and Measures		
Variable	Surrogate	Measure
Predictor:		
National Culture	Power Distance Uncertainty Avoidance Individualism Masculinity	(Outcomes)
Managerial biases	Stereotyping	
Criterion:		
Implementation of management theory	(1a) Presence of Employee Involvement or (1b) Absence of Employee Involvement (2) If *1a* exists, then level of involvement	Likert Scale

Surrogates for the Predictor Variable

The implied predictor variables, although not being tested, were national culture and managerial stereotyping. Other variables, such as inability of the manager to implement employee involvement methods and numerous other reasons for failure to implement, were assumed to be present. Surrogates for the primary variables were Hofstede's (1980a) four value dimensions for national culture and stereotyping for the bias variable (See Table 1).

RESEARCH DESIGN

To test the hypothesis, a comparative analysis approach was chosen. This comparison was made between pairs of United States managers employed by *maquiladora* companies (e.g., each Mexico-based expatriate manager working for a particular company was compared to the United States-based home country national manager employed by the same company). Individuals in the simple random sampling were sent research instruments soliciting information about their management style and demographic information. Results were gathered from an initial mailout and numerous followups. The procedure used to test the hypothesis was the Wilcoxon matched-pairs signed-ranks test. Other statistical procedures were used to draw further conclusions.

Comparative Analysis

A comparative research design was selected for this study. United States- and Mexico-based managers responses to the questions on the Likert-type questionnaire were compared to determine the extent to which they practiced employee involvement. If they used a participative style, the scale differentiated between a consultative-participative style (lower level of participation) and a participative-group style (higher level of participation); therefore, it was possible to compare levels of participation between individual pairs and among the pairs for each question on the scale.

Conclusions were drawn concerning whether or not each of the managers in every pair of companies (United States and Mexico) engaged in employee involvement practices, and, if participation was practiced, the direction of the level (lower or higher) of participation.

The control provided by the comparison of United States parent companies and their Mexico subsidiaries was a powerful factor. If, for example, a parent company utilized a participative style of management with a domestic workforce but did not practice a participative style in their subsidiary Mexican plants with a host country workforce, there were more inferences to be drawn than if the two companies had been independent of one another. Thus, the strength of the assumptions that could be made were stronger with dependent samples than with independent samples.

SIMPLE RANDOM SAMPLING

The sample for this study consisted of forty matched pairs of company-plant facilities conducting business in the *maquiladora* industry (a total of eighty managers). The United States companies were manufacturers that operated subsidiary assembly plants in Mexico. United States parent companies were primarily from the Mexican border areas of Texas, Arizona, and California, but some larger companies were located in the northern United States. The subsidiary assembly plants were also clustered along the Mexico-United States border in the Mexican states of Chihuahua, Coahuila, Nuevo Leon, Baja California Norte, and Sonora, except for a few that were dispersed further into the interior of Mexico.

A sampling of 500 paired *maquiladora* companies was randomly selected from a population of more than 2,000 companies. This number--2,000--represented the entire population of the *maquiladora* industry as of July 1991. Questionnaires were mailed to 500 parent plants in the United States and to their 500 subsidiary assembly plants in Mexico; a follow-up was conducted six weeks later. After the final faxed request, approximately two weeks was allotted for the return of questionnaires. At the end of this period, 40 parent companies and their subsidiaries had been matched for a total sample of n=40 pairs. (Completed questionnaires received after this point were not included in the sample, even though they may have constituted a pair).

A recently published directory (June 1991) of the *maquiladora* industry provided the population. *The Complete Twin Plant Guide* (1991, iii) is "a directory of the approximately 2,000 twin plants now operating throughout Mexico and the United States. . . . It is intended as a reference source and as a tool for facilitating research . . . within this industry." The set is divided into three volumes--North and South Baja California (Volume I), Central Corridor Region: Chihuahua, Sonora & Other Central/Pacific States (Volume II), and Rio Grande, Gulf and lower Pacific Region: Coahuila, Nuevo Leon, Tamaulipas and Other States in the Gulf of Mexico (Volume III). The Mexican regions border Texas, New Mexico, Arizona, and California in the United States.

Each alphabetical listing in the directory includes the name of the assembly plant in Mexico, the physical or mailing address, telephone and fax numbers, the name of the plant manager, the size of the plant, the number of employees, and the product assembled. Also included are the U.S. parent company name, address, and telephone number.

Numbers were assigned to the alphabetical listing of pairs of *maquiladora* plants, beginning with Volume I (pair number 1) and sequentially proceeding through Volumes II and III, until pair number 500 was reached. Numbers generated by the random number procedure were then matched to those in the three volumes.

MEASUREMENT INSTRUMENT

The test instrument used was a derivation of Rensis Likert's (1967) *Profile of Organizational Characteristics* (*POC*) instrument. Likert's instrument, which was developed and tested for reliability and validity in the 1960s, was published in his 1967 book, *The Human Organization*. Since that time, numerous researchers have used the instrument in their research, and the scale type has become a universal format for measurement.

Description of the Scale

In its original form, Likert's scale included fifty-one categorized questions pertaining to managerial styles. (Refer to Appendix A for Rensis Likert's Original *POC* scale). The questionnaire derived for this research modified twenty-two of the 51 constructs from the original scale primarily by changing much of the wording to terms more commonly used today; e.g., "subordinate" was replaced with employee, "superior" with manager.

The rationale for selecting these particular 22 variables was twofold. First, it was believed that plant managers would more readily respond to a shorter version of the scale than to the original, long version (i.e., a 22 question scale reduced the number of letter-size pages from approximately thirteen to only five). Secondly, through a reduction process, it was possible to select those variables that were deemed most descriptive of employee involvement practices (e.g., the question types from the original scale that dealt specifically with "groups" or teamwork were chosen for the modified version used in this study).

Likert's *POC* scale, sometimes referred to as the *System 4* scale, measures four types of managerial styles or systems. This ordinal scale ranges from exploitative authoritative (*System 1*) to benevolent authoritative (*System 2*) to participative consultative (*System 3*) to participative group (*System 4*), with five possible ranking in each of the four categories (i.e., least to most agreement).

The *System 4* style is the most highly participative of the two employee involvement styles. Likert advocated this style, which is parallel to current employee involvement theory. For example, Likert (1961, 15) discussed "favorable, cooperative attitudes existing throughout the organization that exhibit mutual trust and confidence." He also referred interchangeably to groups and group work. Several questions on the *POC* scale query respondents about group work and cooperation.

Categories of Rating Scale Items

The twenty-two questions modified for in this study were categorized as follows: Category 1 is related to leadership processes; category 2, communication; category 3, attitudinal, motivational, and perceptual; category 4, interaction-influence; and category 5, decision making. Managers in the *maquiladora* plants were asked to indicate the degree to which they held an opinion about each of the questions in the five categories.

Category 1--Leadership Processes

The first category concerns organizational leadership processes and determines the extent to which managers and employees have confidence and trust in each other; the extent to which managers behave so that employees feel free to discuss important aspects of their jobs; and the extent to which immediate managers try to get employees' ideas and opinions in solving job problems.

Category 2--Communication Processes

The second section contains questions about the amount of interaction and communication aimed at achieving the organizations objectives, direction of information flow, extent to which managers willingly share information with employees, and accuracy of upward communication.

Category 3--Attitudinal, Motivational, and Perceptual Processes

The third section contains questions related to attitudes, perceptions, and motivational stimuli; the psychological closeness of managers to employees; how well managers know and understand problems faced by employees; and the accuracy of their perceptions.

Category 4--Interaction-Influence Processes

The fourth category is devoted to interaction-influence processes within the organizations. Questions concern the amount and character of interaction, amount of cooperative teamwork present, extent to which employees can influence the goals, methods, and activity of their units and departments (as seen by managers and as seen by employees), and amount of actual influence which managers can exercise over the goals, activity, and methods of their units and departments.

Category 5--Decision-making Processes

Questions in the fifth category query subjects about the character of decision making in the organization and the level at which organizational decisions are made. It also includes the adequacy and correctness of information available for decision making, the extent to which decision makers are aware of problems, the degree to which employees are involved in work-related decisions, and whether decision making is based on one-to-one or team patterns of operation.

Rationale for Selection of Instrument

Likert's *System 4* instrument was selected as a model for this research for several reasons: (a) Its long-term usage and continual revalidation have made it a classic instrument. (b) It was important to determine the actual managerial style being practiced by plant managers rather than their beliefs about management practices. Likert (1961, 11) advocates directing respondents "to describe their own organization as they experience it," *rather than as they think it should be.* (c) The resemblance between Likert's participative group (*System 4*) and current approaches to participation made this classic instrument ideal for measuring the implementation of employee involvement practice methods in the U.S.-Mexico *maquiladora* industry.

PROCEDURES FOR THE
COLLECTION OF DATA

The first step in collecting data was to mail a questionnaire and a list of questions seeking demographic data to each of the companies in the 500-paired sample. A cover letter contained an introduction to the study, stated the purpose of the study, and briefly discussed the significance of the research. As an incentive to respond, two commitments were made to the prospective respondents: (a) to provide anonymity of the companies and respondents, excluding persons involved in the research project; and (b) to furnish the results of the study to the respondents. Also included in the initial mailout was a self-addressed, coded, and stamped return envelope. No time limit for return of the questionnaires was designated in either the U.S. or Mexico mailing because of the unreliability of the Mexican mail service.

A second letter and questionnaire were mailed six weeks later to the plant managers whose affiliates had responded (ninety-six managers). It was assumed that the address printed in the directory was accurate if one company out of the pair had responded. The second mailing was an effort to maximize the response rate by increasing the matching probability (the probability of matching a pair from 1,000 companies was very low). The original mailout resulted in an 11.4 percent return rate, and only 8 percent of the returns were paired.

Approximately three days after the follow-up letters were mailed, an intensive follow-up campaign was initiated. Each of the 96 managers was called and a short message was left urging him or her to respond. During the telephone call, the address, fax number, and the managers' name and title were verified. The next phase began four or five days later, after the managers had an opportunity to respond to the message. Managers who had still not returned the questionnaire were sent another follow-up letter and questionnaire. In the third phase of the campaign, questionnaires were faxed to managers who had not responded. This contact method proved to be the most successful--the response rate was highest to the faxed requests.

At the time the data files were closed, two weeks after the instruments were faxed to non-responding managers, managers in eighty companies (i.e., 40 pairs) had responded. (Refer to U.S.- Mexico map of 40 companies in the sample on page 69. *Map Notation*: The circled numbers "19" refer to a particular MNC headquartered in the Northern U.S. with *maquiladora* assembly plant locations in Baja California. The unnumbered map notations refer to the other 39 MNCs in the sample). Several questionnaires, primarily from Mexico, were returned after the cut-off date; therefore, these were not included for the comparative analysis. Questionnaires were coded as they were returned and data were entered into the computerized file.

PROCEDURES FOR THE
TREATMENT OF DATA

The primary statistical procedure used to test data was the Wilcoxon matched-pairs signed-ranks test. Rather than using the parametric matched pairs t-test for hypothesis testing, the Wilcoxon test was selected. The Likert-type scale is an ordinal scale (Champion 1981, 168) and requires a nonparametric measure. The samples were dependent, and the Wilcoxon test is the appropriate nonparametric procedure for testing dependent, matched-pair samples.

Because the hypothesis was one-tailed, and because additional information could be gained by learning the direction of any differences in the ranked pairs, a one-tailed rather than a two-tailed Wilcoxon was selected. The Wilcoxon test also yields a p-value or achieved significance level. The alpha (significance) level was set at $p<0.05$.

Other statistical measures were also used in testing the data. A correlation analysis was conducted on the responses. Correlation coefficients were determined by using Spearman's rho rank

Figure 1. U.S. - Mexico Maquiladora Matched Pair Sample

(40 Matched Pairs)

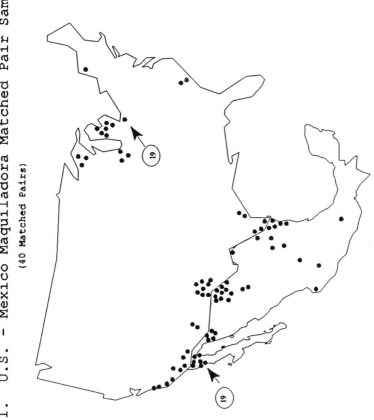

correlation test. Contingency tables were constructed to cross-tabulate demographic data with level of participation on selected questions from the instrument. Finally, additional statistics were obtained for the contingency tables to determine the relationship between cross-tabulated variables.

PROCEDURES FOR INTERPRETING THE DATA

The statistical procedures used provided initial insight into the problem by determining whether the hypothesis would be rejected or would fail to be rejected. The p-value indicated the significance of these results. Once these determinations were made, conclusions were drawn.

LIMITATIONS OF THE STUDY

An initial limitation arose from the inability to study this problem under laboratory or field experimental conditions. However, due to a) the fact that the *maquiladora* industry is so widespread (United States plants concentrated along the Mexico-United States border and extending into many of the northern U.S. states, and Mexican plants also with close proximity to the Mexico-United States border and ranging into the interior regions of Mexico), and (b) very limited access to Mexican assembly operations (e.g., Mexican *maquiladora* plants, even though usually United States owned, do not openly welcome visitors due to sensitivities concerning wages, pollution, and living conditions of the Mexican workers), it was not feasible to apply a purely experimental design.

The necessity of using a mailed survey instrument for the collection of data provided a second limitation. This limitation posed a threat to the internal validity of the study through nonresponse bias. Although the assumption cannot be made that subjects who did not return the questionnaire would have responded the same as those who did reply, there were a number of reasons why questionnaires were not returned: (a) though the most current *maquiladora* industry directory was used (June 1991) some of the addresses had changed or contained inaccuracies. (b) It is also possible that some of the managers did not receive the questionnaire because of the unreliability of the mail in Mexico or because a clerical worker within the organization failed to direct the envelope to the right person. (c) Too, it is also possible that the managers received the questionnaires but, for personal reasons, chose not to answer.

Because the survey was mailed, another threat to internal validity was a systematic response bias. This bias could have been caused by (a) erroneous answers--managers may have responded in a manner to make themselves appear more favorably, (b) answers provided by someone other than the intended recipients, or (c) respondents perceptual interpretations of the questions or terminology that were different from those intended.

Thus, the primary limitations of this study were threats to internal validity. No apparent threats to external validity existed, however. The number of matched pairs (n=40) in the random sample represented a broad cross-section of the *maquiladora* industry, both in the United States and in Mexico. This was true geographically, as well as by industry type. Approximately thirty-eight industry standard industrial classification codes were indicated by the responding managers. These codes were grouped into several general industry types--food processing, metal fabrication, fabrics (auto upholstery and hospital wear), electronic components and fabrication (electrical connectors, television monitors, appliances, switches, ceramic ferrite magnets, automobile harness assemblies, and circuit boards), and ornamental works. The largest concentration of standard industrial classification codes was in the electronic components and fabrication industry, which is also one of the largest industry types in the general *maquiladora* industry population. (Refer to Appendix C).

IV

Results of Statistical Analyses

The Wilcoxon matched-pairs signed-ranks test was used for hypothesis testing of the level of employee involvement in United States companies and their Mexican subsidiaries. A correlation analysis was also conducted on the questions from the instrument to determine the degree of association between United States and Mexico paired responses for each question. Correlation coefficients were determined using Spearman's rho rank correlation test. Finally, contingency tables were constructed by cross-tabulating selected demographic data from the information sheet with respondents' participation levels (Systems 1 through 4) on selected questions from the instrument.

WILCOXON MATCHED-PAIRS
SIGNED-RANKS TEST

To test the alternate hypothesis (that the level of employee involvement is greater in United States parent plants than in Mexican *maquiladora* subsidiaries), a one-tailed Wilcoxon matched-pairs signed-ranks test was utilized for each of the 22 questions from the instrument, and the alpha level was set at $p<0.05$. The results of the Wilcoxon test are summarized in Table 2.

Categories of Rating Scale Items	Pairs	Number of Items in Which Null (H_o) Was Rejected	Number of Items in Which Null (H_o) Failed to be Rejected	One-Tailed p-value
Leadership Style variables 5 questions	n= 40	0	5	0.1343 0.0724 0.1154 0.2601 0.3407
Character of communication process variables 4 questions	n= 40	2	2	0.2145 0.0415 0.0116 0.1260
Attitudinal, motivational perceptual variables 3 questions	n= 40	0	3	0.1903 0.3240 0.0845
Interaction-influence/ level of cooperation variables 5 questions	n= 40	2	3	0.7480 0.0176 0.3981 0.0435 0.2051
Character of decision making process variables 5 questions	n= 40	0	5	0.2329 0.1917 0.2602 0.2531 0.2536

Test statistics were statistically significant (<0.05)

Only 4 of the 22 questions from the instrument indicated a significant (<0.05) difference (i.e., the null hypothesis was rejected for questions II-2, II-3, 6-3, and 6-C2). (See Table 3). For the other 18 questions, there was not sufficient evidence to reject the null form of the hypothesis.

Table 3.--Partial Test Statistics of the Four Organizational Variables that Showed a Significant Difference at the <0.05 Level			
Variable	Mean Difference	SD	One-Tailed *p*-value
Communication 1	-6.42	22.84	0.0415
Communication 2	-8.30	22.21	0.0116
Interaction/influence 1	-7.72	22.40	0.0176
Interaction/influence 2	-6.35	22.87	0.0435

n=40

Two of the 4 questions that indicated significant differences between the United States and Mexico managers' (U.S. and U.S. expatriates in Mexico) responses compared the direction of information flow in the organization; a third compared the amount of cooperative teamwork present; and the fourth compared the extent to which employees believed they could influence the goals, methods, and activities in their departments and/or teams. Table 4 contains a list of the four questions and the variables they represented. A higher level of participation in the United States parent company than in the Mexican subsidiary was indicated by a significantly higher average score for United States companies on these four questions.

Variables	System 1 Exploitative authoritative	System 2 Benevolent authoritative	System 3 Partici-pative consulta-tive	System 4 Partici-pative group
Table 4.--Description of the Four Variables in which U.S. Managers Indicated Significantly Higher Levels of Employee Involvement than U.S. Managers in Mexico				
Direction of information flow.	Downward	Mostly Downward	Down and up	Down, up, and with peers
Downward communi-cation. Extent to which managers share infor-mation with employees.	Provide minimum of information	Give employees only information manager feels they need	Give informa-tion needed; answer most questions	Seeks to give em-ployees all relevant informa-tion
Amount of cooperation in organiza-tion.	None	Relatively little	Moderate amount	Much through-out company/ plan
Extent to which em-ployees can influence goals, me-thods, and activities of their teams and/or department	None except through informal organization (or union)	Little except through informal organization (or union)	Moderate amount both directly (or through union)	Substan-tial but often indirectly

Thus, based on the results of the test statistic, it was concluded that there were no statistically significant differences between the levels of participation in United States parent companies and their Mexico subsidiaries on 18 of the 22 questions. (See Table 5 for a summary of the 18 organizational variables).

Table 5.--Summary of Eighteen Variables in which There Were No Significant Differences in Levels of Employee Involvement between United States Managers and U.S. Expatriate Managers in Mexico				
Variables	System 1 Exploitative authoritative	System 2 Benevolent authoritative	System 3 Partici- pative consulta- tive	System 4 Partici- pative group
Confidence & trust in employees	None	Almost none	Some- average	Much
Confidence & trust in managers	None	Almost none	Some- average	Much
Managerial support	None	Almost none	Some- average	Much
Employees free to discuss job problems	Not at all free	Not very free	Some- what free	Com- pletely free

Continued on next page

Variables	System 1 Exploitative authoritative	System 2 Benevolent authoritative	System 3 Partici- pative consulta- tive	System 4 Participa- tive group
Managers seek input from employees	Seldom	Sometimes	Usually	Always
Amount of interaction- communi- cation between manager & employee	Very little	Little	Some- average	Much
Amount of upward communi- cation	Very little	Little and cautiously given	Some- average	Much
Interper- sonal relationship between manager & employee	Far apart (very formal)	None- moderate (formal)	Fairly close (some form- ality)	Very close (Friendly, informal)
Manager tries to understand employee's problems	No	Occasion- ally	Usually always	Always

Table 5.--*Continued*

Continued on next page

Variables	System 1 Exploitative authoritative	System 2 Benevolent authoritative	System 3 Partici- pative consulta- tive	System 4 Partici- pative group
Accuracy of perceptions between manager & employee	Often in error	Errors on some	Moderate accuracy	Quite accurate
Amount & nature of interaction between manager & employee	Little with fear	Little	Moderate	Extensive
Extent to which employees have influence as perceived by employee	None	Virtually none	Moderate amount	A great deal
Employees' amount of influence as perceived by manager	Very little	Moderate	Moderate to high	Sub- stantial

Table 5.--*Continued*

Continued on next page

Variables	System 1 Exploitative authoritative	System 2 Benevolent authoritative	System 3 Partici- pative consulta- tive	System 4 Partici- pative group
Level of organiza- tional decision making	All decisions at top	Some minor at lower levels	Most major at top; minor at lower levels	Top- bottom (all levels)
Adequacy of information for decision making at lower levels	Very inadequate	Some adequacy	Adequate	Adequate
Decision makers aware of problems on lower levels	Usually not aware	Some awareness	Usually aware	Very aware
Employees involved in decisions affecting their work	Never involved	Occasionally involved	Usually involved	Always involved
Decision making one-to-one or group pattern facilitating teamwork	One-to-one only	Usually one- to-one	Both; some team- work	Group; teamwork

Table 5.--*Continued*

CORRELATION ANALYSIS

A correlation analysis was conducted on questions from the instrument to determine the degree of association between the responses of paired United States and Mexico companies/ subsidiaries. Correlation coefficients were determined using Spearman's rho to test the strength of the linear relationship between pairs (See Table 6).

Table 6.--Spearman Correlation Coefficients for Significant Paired Responses		
Variable	Correlation Coefficient	*p*-value
Communication 1 (Individual and/or group in achieving company objectives)	0.32848	0.0385
Communication 2 (Direction of information flow)	0.37493	0.0171
Perceptual (Accuracy between manager and employee)	0.48550	0.0015
Decision making (Managerial awareness of problems on lower levels)	0.35565	0.0243

Note: Two-tailed; $p<0.05$; n=40 pairs

All correlation coefficients were positive for the paired responses that were statistically significant, which indicates that the direction was the same. In other words, in each statistically significant paired relationship between a United States parent company and its Mexican *maquiladora* plant, managers in both facilities responded in the same direction on the instrument (i.e., direction, in this case, involves the 1 to 20 ranked scale of the instrument).

The four positive coefficients yielded additional information about the results from the one-tailed, directional Wilcoxon Test. Spearman's rho, a nonparametric technique using data in the form of ranks, was used to determine whether the relationship in paired responses was positive, negative, or zero (no relationship). In the paired responses between United States and Mexico managers, a positive coefficient indicated that high scores were paired with high scores or, conversely, low scores were paired with low scores. For example, if one manager in a matched pair (parent: subsidiary) responded in the upper range on the scale, a positive coefficient indicated that, on the average, the other manager comprising the pair also responded in the higher range of the scale. A pair of managers responding on the lower end of the scale would also be positively correlated. Thus, the four significantly paired relationships with positive coefficients added information about the direction of managers' responses.

CONTINGENCY TABLES

Frequencies were cross-tabulated for certain questions from an information sheet requesting primarily demographic data and the test instrument. The cross-tabulations were repeated separately for the United States and the Mexico plants.

Of particular interest on the information sheet were the questions that directly queried managers about their current or past involvement with participative management practices. Managers' responses to these questions were cross-tabulated in two ways: (a) with other demographic queries from the information sheet and (b) with responses to questions from the instrument.

The first type of comparative analysis is illustrated in Table 7. Responses on the informational question "Did you use any type of participative management in your previous job?" were compared to the informational question "Our plant uses self-managed work teams in which the employee makes decisions affecting production/ assembling or work group outcomes. This type of comparison was made among the U.S. managers and among the U.S. expatriate managers in *maquiladora* assembly plants. In summary, the outcomes for the United States managers showed that 6 of the 20 managers who either strongly agreed or agreed that self-managed work teams were used in their plants had previously practiced some form of participative management in another job. The frequency results for U.S. based managers were similar to those of expatriate managers who strongly agreed or agreed that managed teams were used in their plants--5 of the 19 had previously used participative practices.

Total "yes" and "no" responses to having previously used participative practices differed slightly, however, in comparing the U.S.-based managers to Mexico-based ones. Twenty-one of the 40 (53 percent) United States managers had used participative management prior to their current position, while only 13 of the 40 (33 percent) U.S. expatriate managers had done so.

Once again, similar results occurred when responses to the informational statement--"As participation increases, productivity usually decreases"--and responses to the informational question-- "Did you use any type of participative management in your previous job?"--were compared. Of the 33 United States managers who strongly disagreed or disagreed to the question concerning the relationship between participation and productivity, 15 had previously used participative management. Thirty-six of the expatriate managers strongly disagreed or disagreed to the same question, and of the 36, 23 had used participative management before.

Table 7.--Comparison of Previous and Current Usages of Employee Involvement Practices					
Used Participation Previously	Our Plant Uses Teams				
	Strong Agree	Agree	Not sure	Disagree	Strong Disagree
	U.S.-based Managers				
No (19 total)	7	7	0	5	0
Yes (21 total)	0	6	2	10	3
Cum. totals (40)	7	13	2	15	3
	Mexico-based Managers				
No (27 total)	3	11	3	9	1
Yes (13 total)	3	2	3	3	2
Cum. totals (40)	6	13	6	12	3

When United States and Mexico managers who had practiced participative management in a previous job were asked their opinions on the information sheet about whether participation increases effectiveness, their concurrence was even stronger than in the frequency comparisons of the participation-productivity/previous use of participation. Thirty-six of the 40 United States managers either agreed to strongly agreed that participation increases effectiveness. Seventeen of the 36 had used participative management previously. Of the 40 expatriate managers, 38 either agreed or strongly agreed that effectiveness is the outcome of participation. Twelve of the 38 U.S. expatriate managers supporting effectiveness as an outcome of participation had practiced participative management in a former job.

Other interesting frequency comparisons were made by collapsing the 1 to 20 interval response set on the instrument to Likert's *Systems 1, 2, 3*, and *4*. As in the previous contingency tables, United States managers' and expatriate managers' responses were compared. However, this time, responses to the questions on the information sheet were compared to certain questions from the test instrument. For example, a comparison was made between the informational question "Our plant uses self-managed work teams in which employees make decisions affecting production/assembling or work group outcomes" and one of the questions from the test instrument that showed a significant difference in the hypothesis testing (Amount of cooperation present [in your company facility]). The outcomes of this analysis are shown in Table 8.

Of the 21 United States managers (53 percent of total United States managers) who indicated the highest level of participation (*System 4*) by their responses on the questions from the instrument, 6 (29 percent of the 21) strongly agreed that self-managed work teams were used in their plants. As shown in Table 8, a difference was evident in the responses of Mexico expatriate managers and United States managers. Only 11 Mexico-based managers (28 percent of the total expatriate managers as compared to 53 percent of the U.S.-based managers) responded in the highly participative range (*System 4*). Similar to United States managers, however, 4 of the 11 expatriate managers (36 percent) strongly agreed that self-managed work teams were used in their plants.

The response differences determined by the cross-tabulated frequencies correspond to the findings from the Wilcoxon test. For the question on the instrument concerning the amount of cooperation present, a significant difference was evident at $p=0.0176$. Thus, *in this particular instance*, United States managers indicated significantly higher levels of participation in their plants (a greater amount of employee involvement and teamwork present) than did Mexico-based U.S. expatriate managers.

	Table 8.--Comparison of Amount of cooperation in the Company Facility and the Use of Self-Managed Teams					
	Plant uses Self-Managed Teams					
	Strong Agree	Agree	Not Sure	Disagree	Strong Disagree	Total
	U.S.-based Managers					
System 1 None	0	0	0	0	0	0
System 2 Rela-tively little	0	0	0	2	0	2
System 3 Mo-derate Amount	1	3	2	8	3	17
System 4 Much through out facility	6	10	0	5	0	21
Cum. Total	7	13	2	15	3	40

Continued on next page

	Plant uses Self-Managed Teams					
	Strong Agree	Agree	Not Sure	Disagree	Strong Disagree	Total
	Mexico-based Managers					
System 1 None	0	0	0	0	0	0
System 2 Rela- tively little	1	1	0	3	0	5
System 3 Mo- derate Amount	1	9	5	6	3	24
System 4 Much through out facility	4	3	1	3	0	11
Cum. Total	6	13	6	12	3	40

Table 8.--*Continued*

Neither the United States managers nor the Mexico-based expatriate managers responded to the informational question--Does your plant use self-managed work teams in which the worker makes decisions affecting production/assembling or work group outcomes?--in the same proportion as they responded to the questions from the instrument concerning the amount of cooperation present in their company facility. Twenty-one United States managers indicated a very substantial amount [of cooperation present] throughout the organization but only 16 of these either agreed or strongly agreed that self-managed work teams were used (the other 5 disagreed that self-managed teams were used). The same was true for the U.S. expatriate managers of Mexican plants--11 indicated the presence of a very substantial amount of cooperation but only 7 agreed (or strongly agreed) that self-managed teams were used (of the remaining 4, 1 indicated that they were not sure, and the other 3 disagreed). It can be conjectured from the disproportionate responses to the informational questions and the test instrument questions that the terms "self-managed" or "self-managed teams" connoted a variety of meanings for both the U.S.-based managers and the expatriate managers, and that the connotations were, in some instances, inconsistent with the terms "cooperation" or "cooperative teamwork."

The results of similar cross-tabulation differed slightly from those shown in the previous contingency table (Table 8). A comparison of response frequencies from the demographic question--Our plant uses self-managed work teams in which the worker makes decisions affecting production/assembling or work group outcomes and the test instrument question--(Is decision making based on one-to-one or group pattern facilitating teamwork)--is provided in Table 9. In this case, the majority of responses to the instrument question from the managers in both countries fell within the consultative participative or *System 3 range*. These like responses were congruent with the findings of the Wilcoxon testing--18 of the 22 questions on the instrument showed no statistically significant difference between the implementation of participative management practices in the matched pairs (U.S.-based manager compared to the same company's Mexico-based *maquiladora* plant manager).

However, even though the cumulative responses to the information sheet question for both *System 3* and *System 4* respondents were similar for managers in both countries, a dissimilarity in opinions between the United States managers and the expatriate managers, who scored in the highly participative range (*System 4*), was evident. In this instance, 12 of the United States managers in the *System 4* range agreed or strongly agreed that their plants used self-managed teams, while only 5 of the *maquiladora* plant managers in the System 4 range agreed or strongly agreed that self-managed teams were used.

Although there was lack of agreement between *System 4* respondents in the two countries, there was a general concurrence, overall. The real discrepancy that occurred was analogous to the previous set of contingency table results--more managers in both the United States and Mexico indicated that decision making was based on group patterns of operations (as opposed to one-to-one pattern) than was indicated by the affirmative responses to the question of whether their plant used self-managed work teams. Once again there appeared to be an inconsistency in perception between the term "group" and "self-managed work teams."

An illustration of similar responses from the United States and *maquiladora* expatriate managers is depicted in Table 10. The two variables cross-tabulated in Table 10 are the informational question "Our plant encourages leadership among workers at all levels--from the highest to the lowest level" and the instrument question--"Extent to which immediate manager, in solving job problems, generally tries to get employees' ideas and opinions and make constructive use of them."

Responses from the U.S.-based managers and the Mexico-based ones were comparable on the informational query and the instrument, particularly from managers responding in the *Systems 3* and *4* range. *System 3* responses included 19 United States and 18 U.S. expatriate managers, with 12 of the 19 United States managers either agreeing or strongly agreeing with the informational question. Of the 18 expatriate managers, 10 concurred. Similar response sets occurred in the *System 4* range. Nine United States managers and 7 Mexico

	Plant uses Self-Managed Teams					
	Strong Agree	Agree	Not Sure	Disagree	Strong Disagree	Total
	U.S.-based Managers					
System 1 One-to-One only	0	1	0	0	0	1
System 2 Usually One-to-One	0	1	0	4	0	5
System 3 Both; some team-work	0	6	1	10	3	20
System 4 Group and team-work	7	5	1	1	0	14
Cum. Total	7	13	2	15	3	40

Table 9.--Comparison of Decision-Making Patterns (One-to-One or Group) and Use of Self-Managed Teams

Continued on next page

	Plant uses Self-Managed Teams					
	Strong Agree	Agree	Not Sure	Disagree	Strong Disagree	Total
	Mexico-based Managers					
System 1 One-to-One only	0	0	0	0	0	0
System 2 Usually One-to-One	1	2	0	2	0	5
System 3 Both; some team-work	3	8	5	6	3	25
System 4 Group and team-work	2	3	1	4	0	10
Cum. Total	6	13	6	12	3	40

Table 9.--*Continued*

	Table 10.--Comparison of Leadership Levels and Utilization of Employee Input					
	Plant Encourages Leadership at all Levels					
	Strong Agree	Agree	Not Sure	Disagree	Strong Disagree	Total
	U.S.-based Managers					
System 1 Em-ployee Input Seldom	1	1	0	0	0	2
System 2 Em-ployee Input Some-times	4	3	0	3	0	10
System 3 Em-ployee Input Usually	1	11	3	4	0	19
System 4 Em-ployee Input Always	4	4	0	1	0	9
C u m Total	10	19	3	8	0	40

	Plant Encourages Leadership at all Levels					
	Strong Agree	Agree	Not Sure	Disagree	Strong Disagree	Total
	Mexico-based Managers					
System 1 Em-ployee Input Seldom	0	0	0	0	0	0
System 2 Em-ployee Input Some-times	2	7	5	0	1	15
System 3 Em-ployee Input Usually	3	7	4	4	0	18
System 4 Em-ployee Input Always	3	4	0	0	0	7
Cum. Total	8	18	9	4	1	40

Table 10.--*Continued*

managers responded as being highly participative (*System 4s*). Eight of the 9 United States managers agreed or strongly agreed that their plants encouraged leadership at all levels.

On another comparison made with geographic locations of previous managerial experience with the same instrument question (amount of cooperative teamwork), the results were inconclusive. Nine of the 40 U.S. expatriate managers for previous managers indicated their managerial experience had been with Mexican companies while almost half of the managers in this same group had been on other foreign assignments from the United States companies. Only a few managers responded that they were newly hired.

Additional contingency tables were constructed (Tables 11, 12, and 13) to test the relationship (i.e., through chi-square analysis) between certain demographic questions and instrument items. In these three tables, *System 1-3* response sets were collapsed to obtain valid chi-square analyses. Interesting results for United States managers were found in Tables 11 and 12; although, no relationship of significance existed in the last table (Table 13) for the response sets of either United States or Mexico managers.

As depicted in Table 11, a statistically significant relationship was found to exist for United States managers between responses to the demographic question "Our plant uses self-managed work teams in which employees make decisions affecting production/assembling or work group outcomes" and the instrument item that queried managers about the amount of cooperative teamwork present in their plants. Under the null hypothesis of no relationship, more United States mangers indicating *System 1-3* styles of management disagreed to using self-managed teams than would be expected,

Table 11.--Relationship Between Amount of Cooperative Teamwork and the Use of Self-managed Teams		
	Plant Uses Self-Managed Teams	
	Agree/Strongly Agree	Disagree/strongly Disagree
U.S.-based Managers		
System 1-3 Cooperative Teamwork (None-Relatively Little-Moderate Amount)	4	13
System 4 (Very substantial amount throughout company)	16	5
Chi-Square=10.45		p=0.0012
Mexico-based Managers		
System 1-3 Cooperative Teamwork (None-Relatively Little-Moderate Amount)	12	12
System 4 (Very substantial amount throughout company)	7	3
Chi-square=1.145		p=0.285

Table 12.--Relationship Between Decision Making Patterns (One-to-one or group) and Use of Self-Managed Teams		
	Plant Uses Self-Managed Teams	
	Agree/Strongly Agree	Disagree/strongly Disagree
U.S.-based managers		
System 1-3 Decision-making patterns (One-to-one only; usually one-to-one; both, some teamwork)	8	17
System 4 Decision-making patterns (group, teamwork)	12	1
Chi-Square=12.477	$p<0.001$	
Mexico-based Managers		
System 1-3 Decision-making patterns (One-to-one only; usually one-to-one; both, some teamwork)	14	11
System 4 Decision-making patterns (group, teamwork)	5	4
Chi-Square=0.001	$p=0.975$	

Table 13.--Relationship Between Leadership Levels and Use of Employee Input		
	Plant Encourages Leadership at all Levels	
	Agree/Strongly Agree	Disagree/strongly Disagree
U.S.-based Managers		
System 1-3 Manager Seeks Input (Seldom-Sometimes-Usually)	21	7
System 4 Manager Seeks Input (Always)	8	1
Chi-Square=0.775		p=0.379
Mexico-based Managers		
System 1-3 Manager Seeks Input (Seldom-Sometimes-Usually)	19	5
System 4 Manager Seeks Input (Always)	7	0
Chi-Square=1.739		p=0.187

while, conversely, more United States managers with a *System 4* style agreed to the presence of cooperative teamwork in their plants. Results for Mexico-based U.S. expatriate managers were insignificant--no relationship was found between the agree/disagree responses and the degree of participation revealed by *System 1-3* and *4*. Findings similar to the previous ones (See Table 11) were discovered through chi-square testing of the relationship between the demographic question (Our plant uses self-managed work teams. . .) used in the prior cross-tabulations and the instrument question "Is decision making based on one-to-one or group patterns of operations?." This second analysis is exhibited in Table 12.

In Table 12, results showed a statistically significant relationship for the responses of United States-based managers to the demographic question and the instrument query. Once again, more U.S.-based managers exhibiting *System 1-3* styles disagreed to using self-managed teams, while more of those with *System 4* styles agreed than would be expected under the chi-square null hypothesis. Also, as in the previous table (See Table 11), no significant relationship existed between the responses of Mexico-based expatriate managers to these particular questions.

In the third cross-tabulations (refer to Table 13), the question "Our plant encourages leadership at all levels" was compared to the instrument question concerning the extent to which managers, in solving job problems, generally tries to get employees' ideas and opinions and make constructive use of them. In this instance, no relationship of significance resulted from the chi-square analysis of response frequencies for either United States or Mexico managers.

The cross-tabulation of variables yielded some important data for facilitating an interpretation of the Wilcoxon's directional results. However, it was also helpful to compare a summary of the responses of Mexico and United States managers to each of the 22 instrument questions (See Table 14).

Table 14.--Summary of Responses to Instrument Questions by United States-based and Mexico-based Managers								
	System 1		System 2		System 3		System 4	
Variables	M	US	M	US	M	US	M	US
Confidence-Trust in Employees	0	0	1	4	34	24	5	12
Confidence-Trust in Managers	3	1	2	5	29	18	6	16
Managerial Support	0	0	6	7	28	17	6	16
Employee Freedom	2	5	7	8	22	13	9	14
Managers Seek Input	0	2	15	10	18	19	7	9
Amount of Communication	1	1	3	3	24	17	12	19
Direction of Information Flow	0	0	13	8	18	14	9	18
Managers Share Information	0	0	10	8	25	15	5	17
Upward Communication	9	7	13	10	15	15	3	8
Interpersonal Relationships	1	2	20	14	13	15	6	9

Continued on next page

	System 1		System 2		System 3		System 4	
Variables	M	US	M	US	M	US	M	US
Managers understand employees' problems	0	0	17	15	14	14	9	11
Accuracy of Perceptions	0	0	3	3	29	21	8	16
Amount of Interaction	0	0	6	5	25	21	9	14
Amount of Cooperative Teamwork	0	0	5	2	24	17	11	21
Amount of Employees' Influence (Managers)	0	0	4	1	23	21	13	18
Amount of Employees' Influence (Employees)	1	1	11	6	22	18	6	15
Amount of Managers' Influence	2	2	8	7	21	17	9	14
Decision Making Levels	2	4	16	12	17	16	5	8
Adequacy of Information	0	0	8	3	24	28	8	9

Table 14.--*Continued*

Continued on next page

Table 14.--*Continued*								
	System 1		System 2		System 3		System 4	
Variable	M	US	M	US	M	US	M	US
Manager Aware of Em- ployees' Problems	1	1	15	14	12	11	12	14
Decision Affecting Em- ployees' Work	0	0	4	5	24	25	12	10
One-to- one or group decision making	0	1	5	5	25	20	10	14
880:880 =1,760	22	27	192	155	486	396	180	302
%880:Mexico 2.50% %880:United States 3.07%			21.82% 17.61%		55.23% 45.00%		20.45% 34.32%	
Combined % 2.78%			19.72%		50.11%		27.39%	

The combined frequencies of both Mexico-based and United States-based managers, as they responded within the ranges of the four systems, suggest that the majority of Mexico and United States companies/subsidiaries practiced some form of participative management, as opposed to authoritative types (*System 1*). Also, it can be assumed that the level of participation was more within the *System 3* range (participation-consultative) for company facilities in both countries. The percentages per country in the highly participative (*System 4*) range were somewhat larger for the United States (34.32 percent) than for Mexico (20.45 percent).

Of the 880 responses from Mexico-based managers, 666 fell within either *System 3* or *System 4*. Almost an equal number, 698 of 880, from United States-based managers fell within either *System 3* or *System 4*. Thus, based on the cumulative data shown in Table 11, there was, with few exceptions, no significant difference between participative practices in the United States parent companies and their Mexican *maquiladora* plants.

SUMMARY

Hypothesis testing utilizing the Wilcoxon matched-pairs signed-ranks test showed no statistically significant differences in 18 of the 22 instrument items tested. Thus, these findings suggested that, in most instances, the level of participation in United States parent companies was not greater than in the Mexican subsidiaries. Results of cross-tabulations between responses from selected information sheet and test instrument questions generally supported these results; although, some interesting differences were found between Mexico and United States *Systems 1-3* and *4* respondents when comparing the current use of self-managed teams in these managers' plants to the degree of cooperative teamwork they believed existed among their workforces.

V

Summary, Conclusions, and Recommendations

This chapter includes a summary of the study and conclusions drawn from the findings. Next, the conclusions are interpreted; and from these interpretations, implications are drawn. Finally, a course of action is recommended for United States expatriates who manage direct investment interests in Mexico--a model was developed to guide the recommended course of action.

The conclusions derived from statistical analyses are divided into two main categories. The first contains the specific participative management research problem as delineated by the hypothesis in this study: If a U.S. multinational is utilizing employee involvement (EI) management strategies in its domestic facilities--U.S. manager and a U.S. workforce--is the company able to transfer these EI strategies to its *maquiladora* assembly plants in Mexico--a U.S. expatriate manager managing a Mexican workforce. Yes or No? If the response is "yes," is the level of participation more or less in the Mexican *maquiladora* subsidiary?

Following a summary of the conclusions, further interpretations are made and implications pertaining to three subject areas are drawn. (a) *Management theory implementation*: What was learned about the implementation of employee involvement practices from parent company to foreign subsidiary? Is there a natural corollary between parent and subsidiary? That is, if participation is practiced in a parent company, can the assumption be made that it will also be practiced in a subsidiary? (b) *Employee involvement practices*: Do some Mexican assembly plants practice participation when their parents do not? Are there correlations between the use of participative practices and the size of a plant, its geographic location, or how long the plant manager has been in a managerial position? Is there a positive correlation between a manager's current use of participation and his or her previous experience with EI? Are employee involvement practices being used as pervasively in MNCs as the current literature suggests? Is the contemporary use of the term "self-managed work team" congruent with the actual practice of participation or employee involvement? (c) *Trade pacts, such as the North American Free Trade Agreement*: If employee involvement practices are advocated by a U.S. multinational, what are the implications for additional United States direct foreign investment in Mexico and, thus, the transference of an EI philosophy?

After these questions are answered, recommendations are offered--a model is drawn to graphically illustrate the recommended suggestions for U.S. firms seeking direct foreign investment opportunities in Mexico, especially for those firms capitalizing upon the openings being provided by NAFTA.

SUMMARY OF THE STUDY

Matched pairs of United States parent companies (MNCs) and their Mexican subsidiaries were studied to determine the level of employee involvement in each. It was hypothesized that United States plants (i.e., U.S. home country national managers and U.S. domestic workforces) would have higher levels of employee involvement than would Mexico plants (i.e., U.S. expatriate managers and Mexico host country workforces). In order to examine this premise, United States managers on both sides of the border were surveyed using an instrument that queried them in four organizational categories--decision making, communication, interaction-influence, and attitudinal-motivational-perceptual characteristics.

After responses were obtained from each of the eighty managers in the random sample (forty matched pairs of companies/managers), the hypothesis was tested using the Wilcoxon matched-pairs signed-ranks test. Results indicate that in eighteen of the twenty-two instances, no significant difference was evident between the level of employee involvement in the pairs of companies. Thus, in this study, the prevailing premise--that management theory cannot be readily transferred and, thus, implemented under cross-cultural conditions--was not supported in the majority of situations.

CONCLUSIONS

From the forty paired responses, eighteen of the twenty-two questions on the test instrument revealed no significant difference in levels of employee involvement between United States parent companies in the *maquiladora* industry and their Mexico subsidiaries. In only four instances was the level of participation in United States parent companies more than in their Mexican assembly plants. The four questions revealing a significant difference were from two of the five categories on the scale that pertained to communication processes (category 2) and the interaction-influence processes (category 4) within the organization (see Table 4). The other three categories (i.e., leadership process variables; attitudinal, motivational, and perceptual variables; and decision making processes) showed no significant differences (see Table 6).

Level of Participative Management

Thus, based on hypothesis testing, it was concluded that, for the paired sample (n=40), there was seldom any significant difference in the levels of participation in United States parent *maquiladora* companies and their Mexico subsidiaries. Organizational leadership processes, decision making processes and one other set of organizational variables all indicated no statistically significant differences. Only four questions involving communication and interaction-influence relationships showed that the participation level was higher in United States parent companies than in Mexican *maquiladora* subsidiaries.

Implementation of Theory United States to Mexico

Using the results of hypothesis testing in conjunction with contingency table outcomes it was possible to derive conclusions concerning the criterion variable of management theory implementation. Employee involvement practices are being implemented in the *maquiladora* assembly plants in Mexico by expatriate managers using host country workforces.

IMPLICATIONS

Further interpretation of the conclusions and implications of these for employee involvement practices and increased direct foreign investments in Mexico as a result of major trade accords (e.g., currently, the North American Free Trade Agreement and the General Agreement on Tariffs and Trade, if the latter is ratified by the two countries) are included in the following sections.

Transferability Issue and EI

Management theory, in this case participative or employee involvement theory, was being implemented, to some degree, from United States parent companies to their Mexico subsidiaries. The summary of responses from the instrument (see Table 14) shows that a far greater number of Mexican assembly plant managers were practicing either a *System 3* or *System 4* style of participation than were using an authoritative style. No assumptions can be made, however, about a natural corollary existing between a parent company and a subsidiary in the usage of participative styles versus the other two authoritative styles (i.e., one cannot assume that because participation is practiced in the United States parent company that it is necessarily practiced in the Mexican subsidiary). In a large number of pairs in the sample, both parent and subsidiary practiced participative methods. However, there were several instances in which the United States parent practiced participation and the Mexican subsidiary did not; in some pairs, the Mexican subsidiary practiced participation and the United States parent company did not.

The implication for the transferability issue is that, in the case of the United States and Mexico's *maquiladora* industry, it is not a valid concern. Hofstede (1980a) suggests that Mexico differs in three of four value dimensions from the United States. The power distance dimension is particularly pertinent to this study and to the implementation of participative practices in Mexico. Hofstede's premise, briefly recapitulated, is that persons in the United States have a relatively small power distance (i.e., because a basic belief in equality exists, employees typically see very little distance between themselves and their managers), while persons in Mexico have a high power distance. Mexican employees typically perceive a large distance between themselves and their managers and typically seek to further enlarge this distance, according to Hofstede's theory. The inference from this theory is that the employee involvement model, which works to decrease power distances, is in opposition to Hofstede's theory about Mexican workers.

Thus, as Hofstede's theory pertains to this study, there could exist a problem with the implementation of employee involvement practices by United States managers in Mexico due to incongruity among values; however, the present findings dispute that premise.

A similar study also contradicted Hofstede's premise: Podsakoff et al.'s (1986) compared Mexican employees to United States employees on leader behaviors. Podsakoff et al. found that, despite national boundaries, there was a substantial degree of similarity in the way Mexican and United States employees dimensionalized certain leader behaviors.

In summary, the present study is not congruent, within United States-Mexico *maquiladora* parameters, with transferability theories conceptualized by Adler (1983a); Adler and Jelinek (1986); Bhagat and McQuaid (1982); Boyacigiller and Adler (1991); Bronson (1994); Butler and Teagarden (1993); Doktor, Tung, and Von Glinow (1991b); Hofstede (1980a, 1983a, 1983b, 1984a, 1987, 1991); Laurent (1983); Schneider (1988); Triandis (1982-1983) and Tung (1993). Moderate to high levels (*System 3* to *System 4*) of participative management are being implemented by United States expatriate managers in the Mexican *maquiladora* subsidiaries of United States companies.

Degree of Implementation of EI

Current literature in the field of management suggests that employee involvement practices are increasingly being utilized in the United States. A recent survey reported that more than one-third of the United States businesses studied plan to increase participation by implementing quality-related teams within the next three years (Ernst and Young and American Quality Foundation 1991). In the present study, 77.50 percent of the total responses from both Mexico and United States managers fell within the *System 3* or *System 4* participative categories (see Table 11). This statistic correlates positively with the current popular literature.

A second aspect of contemporary thought concerning employee involvement is the terminology used to describe the highly participative practices that are being utilized in many organizations today. The terms used most often are cross-functional work teams and self-managed work teams. However, in a cross-tabulation between responses to the demographic item "our plant uses self-managed work teams" and the instrument question "what is the amount of cooperative teamwork present in your plant?" an inconsistency was found in the responses for both the United States managers and the Mexico managers. Of the twenty-one United States managers who indicated a "very substantial amount of cooperative teamwork' (*System 4*) on the question from the test instrument, only sixteen reported that they used self-managed work teams in their plants when queried directly on an "information sheet" requesting additional data about the responding manager; the other five of the twenty-one reported that they did not use self-managed teams (refer to Appendix B for the *General Information Sheet*). The Mexico managers responded similarly--eleven reported a very substantial amount of teamwork on the test instrument but only seven responded in the affirmative on the information sheet to using self-managed teams. Of the remaining four, one indicated a "not sure" on the Information Sheet and the other three indicated they did not use self-managed teams. As conjectured previously, there may be disagreement with the term "self-managed work team" rather than the concept of teamwork.

Another possible explanation is that the words "self-managed" and "cooperative" have different connotations for different people, and that the connotation used in management literature often differs from the connotation used by practitioners in the field. One manager, when asked to describe the method of participative management that he had used in a previous job, replied: "I don't understand the question--I didn't know participative management fell into different categories." Another said: "A modern method from the book *In Search of Excellence*." A third replied: "We used a variation of Nissan's 'Shop Floor Management'; definitely a employee involvement approach but not self-directed." Other descriptors used by the Mexico and United States managers to describe the type of participative management they had used previously were: SPC (Statistical Process Control), PERL (Personal Employee Relations and Leadership), QIS (Quality Improvement Systems), group discussions, worker's committees, team projects, team meetings, matrix, ULINES, team player, task forces or member of task force, modular manufacturing, TQM, cells, and work cells. One manager, for lack of a one-line descriptor, wrote in the margin, "Not enough room here to describe it, I'd need about 50 pages."

The lesson to be learned here seems simple: It is not what people say they do, but what they do that matters. The implication for management theorists who are interested in researching this topic, however, is that precaution needs to be taken when attempting to elicit information from individuals about participative practices. In this study, it was determined from an analysis of the test instrument more managers actually engaged in employee involvement practices--free flow of information, complete trust and confidence, decision making at all levels of the organization--than professed to doing so when queried directly about these on the information sheet.

A third aspect of participation that is very pertinent to this study relates to whether the managers used any type of participative management in prior jobs. (A comparison of United States managers and Mexico managers is included in Table 15).

Table 15.--Summary of Responses Regarding Managers' Use of Participation in Previous Jobs		
Managers	No	Yes
United States	19	21
Mexico	27	13

Of the forty U.S.-based home country managers, 53 percent had used participative management in a previous job. Thirty-three percent of the forty Mexico-based U.S. expatriate managers had used participative management in a previous job. Only conjectures can be made as to why more United States-based managers than Mexico-based managers had previously used participative practices, because no questions were included on the information sheet to query the managers about why they had or had not previously used these practices. Consequently, the relevancy of more managers in the United States having previously used participative management lies in the parent companies' current or future plans to implement employee involvement in Mexican subsidiaries--certainly these practices would be more difficult to implement if the plant managers (the primary managerial position in a *maquiladora* assembly plant) did not have previous experience in participative methods.

One manager of international operations who responded from a large United States manufacturing company that utilized self-managed teams in the United States, offered the following notation:

> We have 17 factories [in Mexico] and today about 10,000 employees. Some plants are more advanced than others. . . Making cultural changes in Mexico is a slow process, but our company has been making significant advances since 1982 [in implementing teamwork].

The Mexico plant manager who responded from the same company had used participative management previously and indicated the use of self-managed teams in the *maquiladora* assembly plant. (As the international operations manager indicated, though, not all of their Mexico plants were as progressive as this one).

Thus, the implication here seems clear: A high level of advocacy of an employee involvement philosophy by the parent company and, thus, the continuing effort to implement participative practices in Mexico were apparently a major reason for the organization's success.

EI Strategies, Enhanced Quality, and Increased Productivity: The Three Cornerstones for Organizational Effectiveness

The finding that participative management practices are being implemented in Mexico has several significant implications for companies that are likely to seek additional direct investment opportunities in Mexico due to the North American Free Trade

Agreement and other future trade alliances (e.g., the General Agreement on Tariffs and Trade).

First, United States manufacturers have been challenged to meet higher standards of product quality, and highly participative practices are thought by many to be integral to doing so. For some, the concepts are synonymous. W. Edwards Deming, for example, has received much acclaim during the last few years for his team-based statistical quality control methods (Walton 1986). He avows that teamwork and quality are inseparable, that the two must go hand-in-hand.

The second implication concerns higher levels of productivity. It has been demonstrated that participative approaches to management increase individual motivation and productivity, thus increasing the overall effectiveness of a firm. This aspect is critical to firms that seek to gain a competitive advantage through *maquiladora* operations or through direct foreign investment (DFI) in Mexico. These moves are made to gain economies of scale, primarily through controlling the cost of labor. Therefore, a paramount question is whether the large, low-wage labor pool that constitutes Mexico's comparative advantage in trade can be "employed involved" on a broad scale; i.e., can the cultural barriers that exist, according to Hofstede and others, be ameliorated or even eliminated so that employee involvement strategies can be widely practiced?

In the 1980s and very early 1990s, the literature, both popular and scholarly, frequently referred to the Mexican workforce as "cheap labor," a term that connoted "poorly trained," "unskilled," and "under educated." *Cheap labor* was definitely a term that did not seem congruent with the concept of employees being involved with organizational decision making. But an article in *Business Week* in 1992 announcing that General Motors was closing factories across the United States and Canada to move operations to Mexico had a new and quite different theme.

> United States auto workers aren't just
> battling Mexico's low wages. They see

themselves pitted against a young, malleable
workforce amenable to the manufacturing
revolution . . . (a flexible labor force, where
highly trained workers in small teams can
jump into each others jobs . . .). In Detroit's
view (GM), Mexico's young workforce
adapts more quickly to new industrial
regimes than entrenched workers. (Baker,
Woodruff, and Weiner 1992, 100)

Since this first eye-opening view of a Mexican workforce
unknown to many, there have been other optimistic testimonies to the
positive attributes of these workers. A United States direct investor
in Mexico has stated: "It is not that [Mexico] laborers are unskilled
or won't make the effort [to achieve high quality]," he explained, "but
rather they lack the proper tools and supervision. With a single piece
of equipment and brief retraining, those workers have not only
improved their job performance but have achieved personal
satisfaction and, down the line, better pay" (Carlin 1994, 25). The
bold, headliner to a cover story article acclaimed: "The Mexican
worker--smart, motivated, cheap--and a potent new economic force
to be reckoned with" (Baker, Smith, and Weiner 1993, 84). The
same article further declares that Mexican workers are a cinch to train
and that they are young and open to new methods. One final
statement by Stevens and Beamish (1993, 83) best summarizes the
emerging new image of the Mexican worker: "The stereotype
foreigners typically have about Mexican workers is no longer valid.
The working population is young and enthusiastic, and ready to
learn."

From these recent depictions of the Mexican worker, a conclusion
can be drawn that the Mexican labor force has the requisite skills to
be participative on the job. This new characterization, coupled with
the findings of this study that employee involvement practices have
been successfully implemented in Mexican *maquiladora*
subsidiaries, portends well for future ventures initiated in Mexico and
the utilization of EI management strategies.

RECOMMENDATIONS

Based on the findings of this study and its underlying theoretical framework, the recommendation to companies actively involved in Mexico's *maquiladora* industry and to companies that will extend their operations there in the future is to implement employee involvement practices, especially highly participative, team-based practices. The positive results of such an endeavor have been previously elucidated; however, the implementation methods could feasibly be problematic. Therefore, a second recommendation is to have two important variables in alignment--a high level of advocacy of an employee involvement philosophy in the parent company and an expatriate plant manager who is fully committed to training and encouraging the host country workforce in this type of participatory management. The consequence of having lesser degrees of either of these important factors is a lower probability that employee involvement management strategies can be successfully implemented. The model shown in Figure 2 more fully describes the ingredients for success.

DISCUSSION

Employee involvement is the contemporary leadership style that seems to have the greatest potential to maximize a firm's effectiveness because individuals within the organization are motivated to perform at their highest levels. Thus, employee involvement is an astute strategy for gaining competitive advantage. It offers a firm the adaptability, flexibility, and innovativeness necessary to compete successfully in a dynamic environment. Fombrun and Wally (1992, 17) affirm that as firms globalize, they ". . . require remarkably adroit leadership able to spearhead the design of flexible corporate configurations and mobilize the commitment of highly diverse employees."

Figure 2. A Model for Implementing Employee Involvement (EI) in a U.S. Managed Firm in Mexico

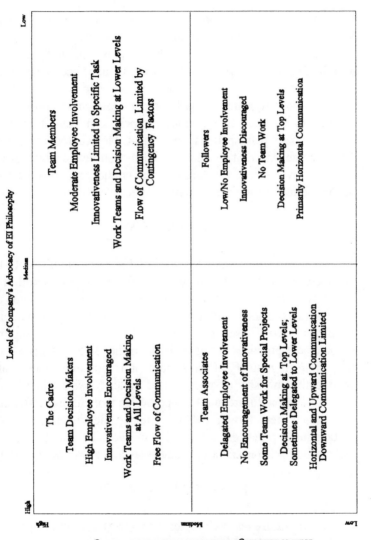

Level of Company's Advocacy of EI Philosophy

High   Medium   Low

The Cadre

Team Decision Makers

High Employee Involvement

Innovativeness Encouraged

Work Teams and Decision Making
at All Levels

Free Flow of Communication

Team Members

Moderate Employee Involvement

Innovativeness Limited to Specific Task

Work Teams and Decision Making at Lower Levels

Flow of Communication Limited by
Contingency Factors

Team Associates

Delegated Employee Involvement

No Encouragement of Innovativeness

Some Team Work for Special Projects

Decision Making at Top Levels;
Sometimes Delegated to Lower Levels

Horizontal and Upward Communication
Downward Communication Limited

Followers

Low/No Employee Involvement

Innovativeness Discouraged

No Team Work

Decision Making at Top Levels

Primarily Horizontal Communication

Level of Expatriate Manager's Commitment to
Train & Encourage Mexican Workforce in EI Strategies

High   Medium   Low

Thus, employee involvement management strategies *can become* a foundation for overall organizational effectiveness with those U.S. companies seeking direct foreign investment opportunities in Mexico. Increased investment flows began to escalate when NAFTA was put into effect on January 1, 1994, and this trend is predicted to continue into the future. "New plant and equipment" have been identified as the most probable investment flows (Hufbauer and Schott 1993, 18).

Consequently, firms that seek direct investment opportunities in Mexico to enhance their competitiveness can benefit from the promulgation of participative management. Mexico, too, can benefit. As expatriate United States managers demonstrate the advantages of employee involvement, the skills to utilize employee involvement will be transferred to Mexican host managers.

SUMMARY

In summary, this study revealed that in eighteen of twenty-two instances, no statistically significant differences were found in the levels of participation of the United States parent companies and their Mexico subsidiaries that comprised the matched-paired random sample (n = 40). These results suggest that implementing employee involvement practices is not an issue in the United States-Mexico *maquiladora* industry. Furthermore, it is possible to generalize beyond this industry to other United States-Mexico alliances that may arise in the future and to hypothesize that cultural differences and biased stereotyping will not impede the implementation of participative practices but will, in fact, be ameliorated by participation's characteristics of democracy and team *esprit de corps*.

FUTURE RESEARCH

Several future research topics emerged as a result of this study. The first topic surfaced from the current popular literature suggesting that members of the Mexican workforce are younger and, thus, more flexible and amenable to participative practices than are many workers in the United States. This suggestion leads to the research question: Are employee involvement practices related to the age of workers? Geographical factors are another topic for consideration. The problem in this instance is whether managers in parent companies in the northeastern United States, separated from the Mexican *maquiladora* subsidiaries by large geographical distances, have different perspectives than managers in the border states of Texas, New Mexico, Arizona, and California. The size of maquiladora facilities may also play a role in the implementation of employee involvement practices. Lastly, a longitudinal study of the present problem to determine whether results change over time would be of interest.

Appendices

Appendix A

Rensis Likert's
Profile of Organizational Characteristics (POC)

Reprinted with permission:

Rensis Likert Associates, Inc.
Consultants in Organization Diagnosis and Human Resource Development
455 E. Eisenhower Pkwy., Suite 15
Ann Arbor, MI 48108
(313) 769-1980; (313) 769-1181 (FAX)

FORM T

PROFILE OF ORGANIZATIONAL CHARACTERISTICS

This questionnaire was developed for describing the management system or style used in a company or one of its divisions.

In completing the questionnaire, it is important that each individual answer each question as thoughtfully and frankly as possible. This is not a test; there are no right or wrong answers. The important thing is that you answer each question the way you see things or the way you feel about them.

INSTRUCTIONS

1. On the line below each organizational variable (item), please place an *N* at the point which, *in your experience*, describes your organization at the present time (*N* = now). Treat each item as a continuous variable from the extreme at one end to that at the other.

2. In addition, if you have been in your organization one or more years, please also place a *P* on each line at the point which, *in your experience*, describes your organization as it was one to two years ago (*P* = previously).

3. If you were not in your organization one or more years ago, please check here ____ and answer as of the present time, i.e., answer only with an *N*.

 Rensis Likert Associates, Inc.

E-1-71

please turn to page 2

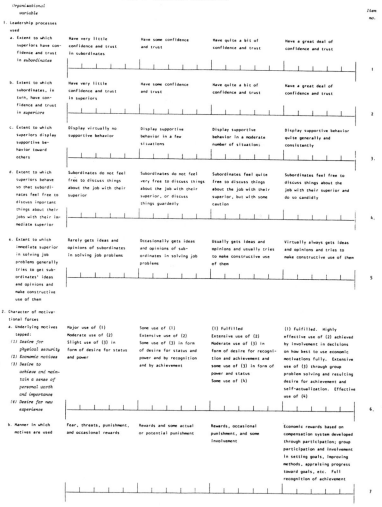

PROFILE OF ORGANIZATIONAL CHARACTERISTICS

PROFILE OF ORGANIZATIONAL CHARACTERISTICS *(Continued)*

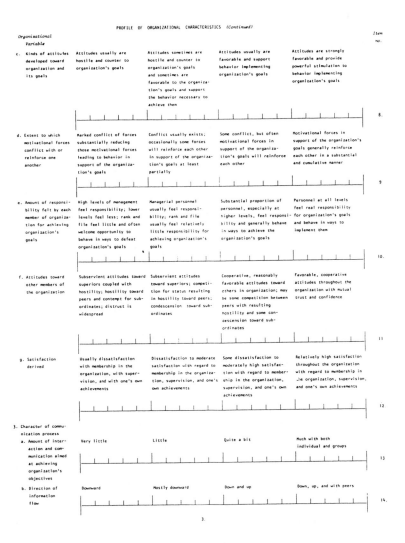

Organizational Variable

c. Kinds of attitudes developed toward organization and its goals

| Attitudes usually are hostile and counter to organization's goals | Attitudes sometimes are hostile and counter to organization's goals and sometimes are favorable to the organization's goals and support the behavior necessary to achieve them | Attitudes usually are favorable and support behavior implementing organization's goals | Attitudes are strongly favorable and provide powerful stimulation to behavior implementing organization's goals |

8.

d. Extent to which motivational forces conflict with or reinforce one another

| Marked conflict of forces substantially reducing those motivational forces leading to behavior in support of the organization's goals | Conflict usually exists; occasionally some forces will reinforce each other in support of the organization's goals at least partially | Some conflict, but often motivational forces in support of the organization's goals will reinforce each other | Motivational forces in support of the organization's goals generally reinforce each other in a substantial and cumulative manner |

9

e. Amount of responsibility felt by each member of organization for achieving organization's goals

| High levels of management feel responsibility; lower levels feel less; rank and file feel little and often welcome opportunity to behave in ways to defeat organization's goals | Managerial personnel usually feel responsibility; rank and file usually feel relatively little responsibility for achieving organization's goals | Substantial proportion of personnel, especially at higher levels, feel responsibility and generally behave in ways to achieve the organization's goals | Personnel at all levels feel real responsibility for organization's goals and behave in ways to implement them |

10.

f. Attitudes toward other members of the organization

| Subservient attitudes toward superiors coupled with hostility; hostility toward peers and contempt for subordinates; distrust is widespread | Subservient attitudes toward superiors; competition for status resulting in hostility toward peers; condescension toward subordinates | Cooperative, reasonably favorable attitudes toward others in organization; may be some competition between peers with resulting hostility and some condescension toward subordinates | Favorable, cooperative attitudes throughout the organization with mutual trust and confidence |

11

g. Satisfaction derived

| Usually dissatisfaction with membership in the organization, with supervision, and with one's own achievements | Dissatisfaction to moderate satisfaction with regard to membership in the organization, supervision, and one's own achievements | Some dissatisfaction to moderately high satisfaction with regard to membership in the organization, supervision, and one's own achievements | Relatively high satisfaction throughout the organization with regard to membership in the organization, supervision, and one's own achievements |

12

3. Character of communication process

a. Amount of interaction and communication aimed at achieving organization's objectives

| Very little | Little | Quite a bit | Much with both individual and groups |

13

b. Direction of information flow

| Downward | Mostly downward | Down and up | Down, up, and with peers |

14.

3.

PROFILE OF ORGANIZATIONAL CHARACTERISTICS *(Continued)*

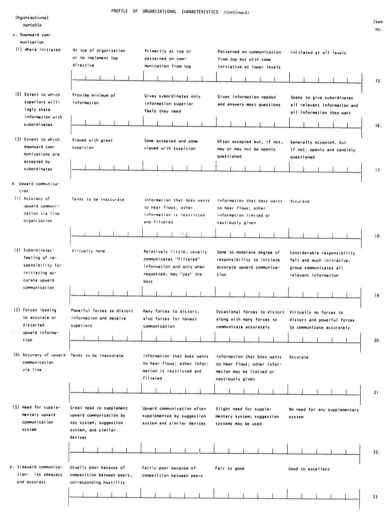

4.

PROFILE OF ORGANIZATIONAL CHARACTERISTICS *(Continued)*

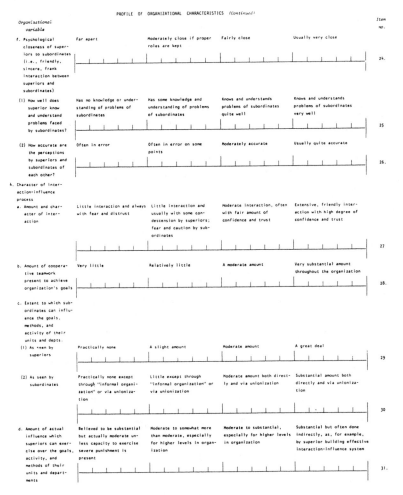

5.

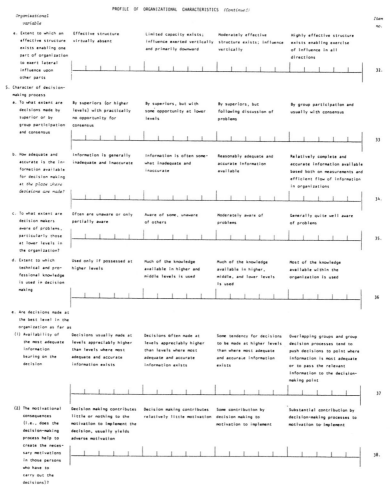

PROFILE OF ORGANIZATIONAL CHARACTERISTICS *(Continued)*

Organizational variable					Item no.
e. Extent to which an effective structure exists enabling one part of organization to exert lateral influence upon other parts	Effective structure virtually absent	Limited capacity exists; influence exerted vertically and primarily downward	Moderately effective structure exists; influence vertically	Highly effective structure exists enabling exercise of influence in all directions	32.
5. Character of decision-making process					
a. To what extent are decisions made by superior or by group participation and consensus	By superiors (or higher levels) with practically no opportunity for consensus	By superiors, but with some opportunity at lower levels	By superiors, but following discussion of problems	By group participation and usually with consensus	33
b. How adequate and accurate is the information available for decision making at *the place where decisions are made?*	Information is generally inadequate and inaccurate	Information is often somewhat inadequate and inaccurate	Reasonably adequate and accurate information available	Relatively complete and accurate information available based both on measurements and efficient flow of information in organizations	34.
c. To what extent are decision makers aware of problems, particularly those at lower levels in the organization?	Often are unaware or only partially aware	Aware of some, unaware of others	Moderately aware of problems	Generally quite well aware of problems	35.
d. Extent to which technical and professional knowledge is used in decision making	Used only if possessed at higher levels	Much of the knowledge available in higher and middle levels is used	Much of the knowledge available in higher, middle, and lower levels is used	Most of the knowledge available within the organization is used	36
e. Are decisions made at the best level in the organization as far as					
(1) Availability of the most adequate information bearing on the decision	Decisions usually made at levels appreciably higher than levels where most adequate and accurate information exists	Decisions often made at levels appreciably higher than levels where most adequate and accurate information exists	Some tendency for decisions to be made at higher levels than where most adequate and accurate information exists	Overlapping groups and group decision processes tend to push decisions to point where information is most adequate or to pass the relevant information to the decision-making point	37
(2) The motivational consequences (i.e., does the decision-making process help to create the necessary motivations in those persons who have to carry out the decisions)?	Decision making contributes little or nothing to the motivation to implement the decision, usually yields adverse motivation	Decision making contributes relatively little motivation	Some contribution by decision making to motivation to implement	Substantial contribution by decision-making processes to motivation to implement	38.

6.

PROFILE OF ORGANIZATIONAL CHARACTERISTICS *(Continued)*

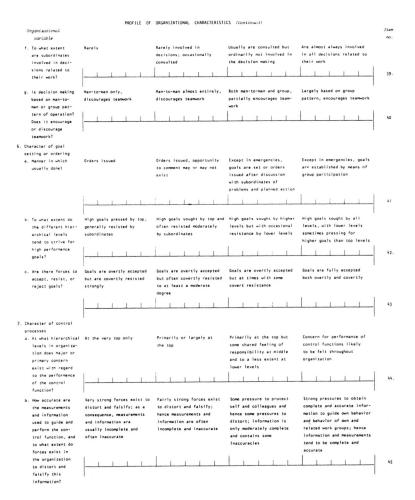

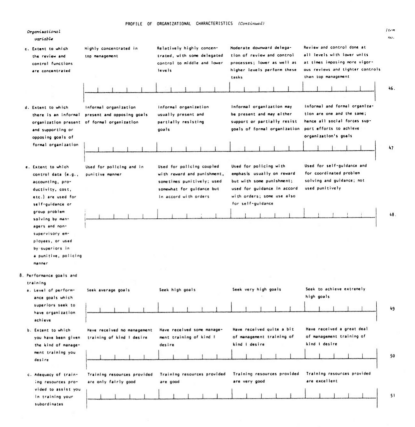

PROFILE OF ORGANIZATIONAL CHARACTERISTICS *(Continued)*

Organizational variable

Item no.

c. Extent to which the review and control functions are concentrated — Highly concentrated in top management | Relatively highly concentrated, with some delegated control to middle and lower levels | Moderate downward delegation of review and control processes; lower as well as higher levels perform these tasks | Review and control done at all levels with lower units at times imposing more vigorous reviews and tighter controls than top management — 46.

d. Extent to which there is an informal organization present and supporting or opposing goals of formal organization — Informal organization present and opposing goals of formal organization | Informal organization usually present and partially resisting goals | Informal organization may be present and may either support or partially resist goals of formal organization | Informal and formal organization are one and the same; hence all social forces support efforts to achieve organization's goals — 47.

e. Extent to which control data (e.g., accounting, productivity, cost, etc.) are used for self-guidance or group problem solving by managers and non-supervisory employees, or used by superiors in a punitive, policing manner — Used for policing and in punitive manner | Used for policing coupled with reward and punishment, sometimes punitively; used somewhat for guidance but in accord with orders | Used for policing with emphasis usually on reward but with some punishment; used for guidance in accord with orders; some use also for self-guidance | Used for self-guidance and for coordinated problem solving and guidance; not used punitively — 48.

8. Performance goals and training

a. Level of performance goals which superiors seek to have organization achieve — Seek average goals | Seek high goals | Seek very high goals | Seek to achieve extremely high goals — 49

b. Extent to which you have been given the kind of management training you desire — Have received no management training of kind I desire | Have received some management training of kind I desire | Have received quite a bit of management training of kind I desire | Have received a great deal of management training of kind I desire — 50

c. Adequacy of training resources provided to assist you in training your subordinates — Training resources provided are only fairly good | Training resources provided are good | Training resources provided are very good | Training resources provided are excellent — 51

8.

Appendix B

GENERAL INFORMATION SHEET

To help interpret the information you gave about your organization, please respond to the following questions.

1. What is your present job title?_____
    How long have you held this position:
    Under a year__ 1-2 years__ 3-5 years__ More than 5 years__

2. How long have you been in a managerial position, whether it was with your present company or some other firm?
    Under a year__ 1-2 years__ 3-5 years__ More than 5 years__

3. What has been the geographic location of your managerial experience?
    U.S. only__ Mexico and U.S.__ Mexico only__ Other?_____
    (Name of location)

4. Are you on foreign assignment in Mexico from a parent *maquiladora* company in the U.S.? Yes__ No__
    If you responded "yes," what was your position with your parent company before being assigned to
    Mexico?_____

5. Is your company's Mexico assembly plant a wholly-owned subsidiary of a U.S. company? Yes__ No__
    If "no," is it a shelter operation? Yes__ No__ Or a subcontracted arrangement? Yes__ No__

6. Does your plant use self-managed work teams in which the worker makes decisions affecting production/assembling or work group outcomes? Yes__ No__

7. a. Did you use any type of participative management in your previous job? Yes__ No__
    b. If "yes" to question "a.," please describe the method:_____

8. What is the size of your *maquiladora* manufacturing plant? Less than 25 employees__ 25-100__ 101-500__ 500-1,000__ 1,000-5,000__

Opinions. Please circle the number that corresponds with your opinion about the statements below. Please use:

1=Strongly agree (SA), 2=Agree (A), 3=Not sure (NS), 4=Disagree (D), 5=Strongly disagree (SD).

		SA	A	NS	D	SD
1.	Our plant uses self-managed work teams in which the worker makes decision affecting production/assembling or work group outcomes.	1	2	3	4	5
2.	Our plant encourages leadership among workers at all levels--from the highest to the lowest level.	1	2	3	4	5
3.	As participation increases, productivity usually decreases.	1	2	3	4	5
4.	Employee participation increases the effectiveness of the workplace/company.	1	2	3	4	5

February 10, 1993

Mr. John Smith
Manager of *Maquiladora* Operations
ABC Manufacturing Corporation
210 Mainway
Detroit, MI 82103

Dear Mr. Smith:

As the manager of a successful plant, you have been chosen to participate in a study that can make an important contribution to knowledge about he *maquiladora* industry an about organizations in general. A number of persons in business and industry agree that a study, such as this one, can be useful to plant managers, like yourself, ant to future managers of direct investments in Mexico.

Your help would really be appreciated. All you need to do is to fill out the enclosed questionnaire and information sheet. The two should only take a few minutes of your time. Your identity will be completely anonymous; only your responses will be included in the data analysis.

If you would like to know what the findings are in this study, just place a check in the upper right-hand corner of the information page. For your convenience in mailing back the questionnaire and information sheet, a stamped, returned envelope is enclosed.

Will you please help?

Thank you for taking your valuable time to invest in this project.

Yours truly,

J. H. Stanford, Researcher

Enc: Stamped, return envelope for mail back to researcher.

FAX COVER SHEET

TO: Mr. John Smith
    Manager of *Maquiladora* Operations
    ABC Manufacturing Corporation

FAX#: (896) 838-0911

FROM: Jane Stanford

DATE: April 15, 1993

SUBJECT: Follow-up to recent request for information

During the past week you received a letter requesting your participation in a research project. You were asked to fill out a series of questions and return them in the enclosed envelope. If you did not have the time to respond earlier, would you do so now? We would really appreciate your help with this project and, in return, we would like to share our findings with you.

Will you take a few moments of your time to give us the information we are seeking? Thank you.

Appendix C

MANUFACTURING PROCESSES (PRODUCTS) OF THE FORTY PAIRS OF *MAQUILADORA* MANUFACTURERS

Vegetable Processing Food Processing	Fruit Cocktail, Frozen
Display Fixtures, Metallic	Frames, Plastic/Metallic
Medical Linens Children's Apparel Leather Works--Gloves	Hospital Caps & Gowns Disposable Hospital Garments
Auto Upholstry	Seat Assembly & Mfg., Auto

Headlights, flashcubes
Garage Door Openers/
   Radio Ctrls/ Electronics
Metal, Brass, Wood Lamps
 	
Electrical Connectors
Electrical Controls
Cable TV Components
TV Monitors
Electrical Motors
Appliances
	Smoke Detectors
	Switches
	Appliance Assembly
	Telephones/Telecommunication
	   Equipment
	Electrical Parts
	Elec. Relays/Components
	Ceramic Ferrite Magnets
	TV Components
	Circuit Boards
	Electronic Filters

Plastic Injection Molding (Wiring) Harnesses--Auto or Assemblies, Elec. Brd.	Grease Guns Chain Gears Machine Shop
Dolls, Plastic	Flower Drying

GEOGRAPHICAL LOCATIONS OF 40 PAIRS
(80 PLANTS)

PARENT COMPANY	BORDER FACILITY	MEXICAN SUBSIDIARY
Cleveland, OH	San Diego, CA	Tijuana, BC
El Monte, CA		Tijuana, BC
Oxnard, CA		Tijuana, BC
San Bernadino, CA		La Mesa, BC
Minnetoka, MI	San Diego, CA	Tijuana, BC
National City, CA		Tijuana, BC
Calexico, CA		Mexicali, BC
City of Industry, CA		Mexicali, BC
San Diego, CA		Ensenada, BC
Dearfield, IL	El Paso, TX	Chihuahua, Chih
Dearborne, MI	Houston, TX	Torreon, Coahuila
Downer Grove, IL	El Paso, TX	Chihuahua, Chih
El Paso, TX		Ciudad Juarez, Chih
Dearborne, MI	El Paso, TX	Ciudad Juarez, Chih
El Paso, TX		Guadalajara, Jalisco
Wells Lamont, IL	El Paso, TX	Ciudad Juarez, Chih
Olive Branch, MS	El Paso, TX	Ciudad Juarez, Chih

Continued on next page

Geographical locations.--Continued		
PARENT COMPANY	BORDER FACILITY	MEXICAN SUBSIDIARY
Someseh, NJ	El Paso, TX	Ciudad Juarez, Chih
Milwaukee, WI	El Paso, TX	Ciudad Juarez, Chih
Minneapolis, MN	El Paso, TX	Ciudad Juarez, Chih
Libertyville, IL	El Paso, TX	Ciudad Juarez, Chih
Tucson, AZ		Ciudad Guadalupe, N.L.
Troy, MI	El Paso, TX	Piedras Negras, Coah
Milwaukee, WI	El Paso, TX	Ciudad Juarez, Chih
Rochester Hills, MI	El Paso, TX	Ciudad Juarez, Chih
Greenville, SC		El Salto, Jalisco
Tucson, AZ	Douglas, AZ	Agua Prieta, Sonora
Greenville, SC		Hermosillo, Sonora
Santa Ana, CA	Nogales, AZ	Nogales, Sonora
Elmhurst, IL	Nogales, AZ	Nogales, Sonora
Walworth, WI		Santa Ana, Sonora
Southfield, MI	McAllen, TX	Saltillo, Coahuila
Houston, TX		Ciudad Acuna, Coahuila
Wheeling, IL		Linares, Nuevo Leon

Continued on next page

Geographical locations.--Continued		
PARENT COMPANY	BORDER FACILITY	MEXICAN SUBSIDIARY
Syosset, NY	Brownsville, TX	Matamoros, Tamulipas
Kalamazoo, MI	McAllen, TX	Matamoros, Tamulipas
Laredo, TX		Nueveo Laredo, Tamulipas
Benton Harbor, MI		Reynosa, Tamulipas
McAllen, TX		Leon, Guanajuata
Dayton, OH		Mexico, D.F.

Appendix D

OUTLINE OF KEY CONCEPTS IN STUDY

I. Competitiveness of U.S. businesses is subject of controversy.
   A.   U.S. manufacturers have lost market and manufacturing shares to Japan and the newly industrialized countries of the Pacific Rim.
   B.   U.S. manufacturers have been challenged by consumers to meet higher standards of product quality and service.

II. U.S. manufacturers must be continuously willing to change in order to meet new competitive demands.
   A.   Must remain innovative.
   B.   Must continue to improve products and processes.
   C.   Must proactively adapt to dynamic environment.

III. Fostering a proactiveness to change requires a special type of organizational structure--an *organic* design.
   A.   The organic structure is relatively flat with few layers of management.
   B.   The organic structure is flexible because rules and policies are replaced by individual decision making throughout the organization.
   C.   The organic structure encourages adaptability and innovativeness through decentralization.

IV. To preserve its key characteristics of adaptability and innovativeness, the organic structure must have compatible management style--an employee involvement form.

A.   Employee involvement is based on egalitarian values.

B.   Employee involvement promotes supportive relationships built on numerous factors
1.   trust between employee and employer.
2.   free flow of communication (vertically and horizontally).
3.   respect for the individual's unlimited capacity to make meaningful contributions to the firm.

C.   Employee involvement has the potential to contribute significantly to the organization's overall effectiveness.

V. A number of contemporary international management theorists argue that a threat exists to utilizing employee involvement in the global arena--transferability problems can arise.

A.   Transferability proponents contend that the successful implementation of management theory by an expatriate firm using a foreign workforce is contingent upon the cultural norms and traditions in the host country being accordant with the underlying assumptions of the theory.

B.   Expatriate managers' biased stereotyping of the host country workforce can also play a major role in transferability.

VI. The problem in this study and its significance hinged on the implementation of employee involvement in a foreign context (Mexico) and this theory's relationship to the success of organizational outcomes and direct foreign investment efforts resulting from trade accords, such as the North American Free Trade Agreement (NAFTA) and the general agreement on Tariffs and Trade (GATT).

A.   The problem in this study
1.   was whether employee involvement practices could be successfully implemented by U.S. mangers in Mexico

subsidiaries with a host country work-force.

2.   tangent to the main problem was one concerned with the negative effects of non-transferability on future direct foreign investment opportunities.

B.   The significance of this study lies in

1.   the positive relationship between employee involvement practices and organizational outcomes.

2.   the implications for U.S. companies that will invest directly in Mexico and manage a host country workforce.

VII.   The scope of this study was limited in three primary directions.

A.   The broad issue of transferability, as conceptualized by contemporary management theorists, was only partially addressed in this study (i.e., only one particular management theory was examined to determine if it could be successfully implemented in a country where cultural values are assumed to be different from those in which the theory has been primarily propagated).

B.   Only two cultures were encompassed--the United States and Mexico as they are represented in the *maquiladora* industry.

1.   The *maquiladora* industry is dichotomously arranged with parent and U.S. assembly plants on the Mexican side.

2.   Some forecasters speculate that as a result of NAFTA, those firms seeking direct investment opportunities in Mexico will emulate the *maquiladora* model (i.e., U.S. technology and capital will be combined with an abundant and low-cost Mexican labor supply).

C. No attempt was made to build a cause and effect relationship (i.e., the intent of the study was to ascertain only whether a specific management theory could be implemented in a foreign culture and not to delve into the reasons for the success or failure of implementation).

VIII. After a review of the literature, a substantive hypothesis was formulated; it stated that employee involvement practices, especially advanced forms that call for teamwork, are not being implemented in the Mexican subsidiaries of U.S. companies by expatriate U.S. managers and a host country work-force. The tested hypothesis (null and alternate) is as follows:

A. H_o: The level of employee involvement in a United States parent company is less than or equal to that of a Mexican *maquiladora* subsidiary.

B. H_a: The level of employee involvement in a United States parent company is more than in a Mexican *maquiladora* subsidiary.

IX. The research design was a comparative analysis between matched pairs of U.S. home country managers in U.S. parent plants and U.S. expatriate managers in Mexican assembly plants.

A. A sampling of 500 pairs of *maquiladora* plants was randomly selected from a population of 2,000 maquiladora companies.

B. Questionnaires were mailed to 500 U.S. parent companies and 500 Mexican subsidiaries; six weeks later, a follow-up was conducted. Both mailings also included demographic queries in the form of an "Information Sheet."

C. Returned questionnaires were matched for a sample of 40 pairs of U.S.-Mexico plant managers.

X. The measurement instrument used was based on Rensis Likert's (1967) scale; 22 questions were modified for the test instrument

for this study. The instrument tested for four managerial styles
or "systems."

A.   *System 4* was referred to by Likert as "participative
group." It represents the highest level of employee
involvement on the scale.

B.   *System 3*, "participative consultative," represented
a lesser amount of involvement than a *System 4*.

C.   *System 2*, "benevolent authoritative," was the least
authoritative of the two systems representing this
style of management.

D.   *System 1*, "exploitative authoritative," was the most
authoritative style.

XI. After the data was collected, the Wilcoxon matched-pairs signed-
ranks test was used to test the hypothesis. Other statistical
measures were correlation analyses, cross-tabulations, and
descriptive statistics.

A.   A one-tailed Wilcoxon matched-pairs signed-ranks
test was conducted on each of the 22 variables from
the instrument and the alpha level was set at
$p<0.05$. *The results of the Wilcoxon were that only
4 of the 22 questions from the instrument indicated
a significant difference ($p<0.05$).*

B.   A correlation analysis was utilized for each of the
22 variables to determine the degree of association
between U.S. and Mexico paired responses.
Correlation coefficients were determined using
Spearman's rho rank correlation test. The four
significantly paired relationships yielded positive
coefficients, which indicated that managers
responded in the same direction on the scaled
questionnaire.

C.   Contingency tables were constructed by cross-
tabulating selected demographic data from the
Information Sheet with respondents' participation
levels (Systems 1 through 4) on selected questions
from the instrument. Finally, chi-square analyses

were performed for the tables to determine the relationship between cross-tabulated variables.

XII.   In summary, statistical testing failed to reject the null hypothesis on 18 of the 22 questionnaire variables. These results, combined with other statistical analyses, suggest that transferability is not an issue among the 40 paired companies comprising the sample in this study--employee involvement is being implemented in Mexican subsidiaries. In some cases, highly participative practices were being implemented by expatriate managers managing Mexican workforces. Furthermore, it is possible to generalize to the *maquiladora* industry as a whole and to other United States-Mexico alliances that may arise in the future and to hypothesize that neither will transferability will not be an issue in these situations.

XIII.   Recommendations for future United States-Mexico alliances are given in the form of a model with level of advocacy from a parent company on the horizontal axis and level of expatriate manager's commitment to train and encourage Mexican workers in EI strategies on the vertical axis.

Bibliography

BIBLIOGRAPHY

Adler, Nancy J. 1983a. Cross-cultural management research:The ostrich and the trend. *Academy of Management Review* 8 (2): 226-232.

_____. 1983b. A typology of management studies involving culture. *Journal of International Business Studies* 14, 2 (Fall): 29-47.

_____. 1986. *International dimensions of organizational behavior.* Belmont, California: Wadsworth, Inc.

_____. 1991. *International dimensions of organizational behavior.* 2nd ed. Boston, Massachusetts: PWS-Kent Publishing Company.

Adler, Nancy J., and John L. Graham. 1989. Cross-cultural interaction: The international comparison fallacy? *Journal of International Business Studies* 20, 3 (Fall): 515-537.

Adler, Nancy J., and Mariann Jelinek. 1985. Is 'organizational culture' culture bound? *Human Resource Management* 25 (1): 73-90.

Agosin, Manuel, and Francisco J. Prieto. 1993. Trade and foreign direct investment policies: Pieces of a new strategic approach to development? *Transnational Corporations* 2, 2 (August): 63-86.

Ajiferuke, M., and J. Boddewyn. 1970. Culture and other explanatory variables in comparative management studies. *Academy of Management Journal* 13 (April): 153-163.

Ali, Abbas, M. Al-Shakhis, and S. Nataraj. 1991. Work centrality and individualism: A cross-national perspective. *International Journal of Manpower* 12, (1): 30-38.

Areck, Pamela L., and Robert B. Settle. 1985. *The survey research handbook.* Homewood, IL: Richard D. Irwin, Inc.

American auto makers need major overhaul to match the Japanese--They may have to streamline product development, gain worker flexibility. 1992. *The Wall Street Journal*, 89, 7 (10 January): A10.

Anderson, Lynn R. 1983. Management of the mixed-cultural work group. *Organizational Behavior and Human Performance* 31 (June): 303-330.

Ansoff, H. Igor. 1988. *The new corporate strategy*. New York: John Wiley & Sons, Inc.

Argyris, Chris. 1957. *Personality and organization: The conflict between the system and the individual*. New York: Harper & Row.

Asheghian, Parviz, and Bahman Ebrahimi. 1990. *International business-economics, environment, and strategies*. New York: Harper Row, Publishers.

Atiyyah, Hamid S. 1994. Workplace democracy under an authoritarian regime: A case study. *Organization Development Journal* 12, 1 (Spring): 1-8.

Austin, James E. 1990. *Managing in developing countries-strategic analysis and operating techniques*. New York: The Free Press.

Babbie, Earl R. 1973. *Survey research methods*. Belmont, CA: Wadsworth Publishing Company, Inc.

Bacon, Kenneth H. 1993. Trade pact is likely to step up business even before approval--U.S. exports are expected to rise, and companies to expand investments. *The Wall Street Journal*, XC, 32 (13 August): A1, A10.

Baker, Stephen, David Woodruff, and Elizabeth Weiner. 1992. Detroit south--Mexico's auto boom: Who wins, who loses. *Business Week* 16 March, 98-103.

Baker, Stephen, Geri Smith, and Elizabeth Weiner. 1993. The Mexican worker--Smart, motivated, cheap--and a potent new economic force to be reckoned with. *Business Week* 19 April, 84-92.

Barcelo, John J. 1991. A history of GATT unfair trade remedy law--Confusion of purposes. *World Economy* 14, 3 (September): 311-333.

Barnett, Carole K. 1987. Men and Women of the corporation revisited: Interview with Rosabeth Moss Kanter. *Human Resource Management* 26, 2 (Summer): 257-23.

Barnum, Cynthia, and Natasha Wolniansky. 1989. Why Americans fail at overseas negotiations. *Management Review* 7 (October): 55-58.

Bartlett, Christopher A. 1986. Building and managing the transnational: The new organizational challenge. In *Competition in global industries,* ed. by Michael E. Porter, 121-142. Boston Mass: Harvard Business School Press.

Bartlett, Christopher A., and Sumantra Ghoshal. 1987a. Managing across borders: New strategic requirements. *Sloan Management Review* 28, 4 (Summer): 7-17.

Bartlett, Christopher A., and Sumantra Ghoshal. 1987b. Managing across borders: New organizational responses. *Sloan Management Review* 29 (1): 45-53.

Bartlett, Christopher A., and Sumantra Ghoshal. 1988. Organizing for worldwide effectiveness: The transnational solution. *California Management Review* 31 (1): 54-74

Bartlett, Christopher A., and Sumantra Ghoshal. 1992a. *Transnational management-text, cases, and readings in cross-border management.* Homewood, IL: Richard D. Irwin, Inc.

Bartlett, Christopher A., and Sumantra Ghoshal. 1992b. What is a global manager? *Harvard Business Review* (September-October): 124-132. Bass, Bernard M. 1990. *Bass & Stogdill's handbook of leadership-theory, research, and managerial applications.* 3rd ed. New York: The Free Press.

Bass, Bernard M., P. C. Burger, R. Doktor, and G. V. Barrett. 1979. *Assessment of managers: An international comparison.* New York: The Free Press.

Batres, Roberto E. 1991. A Mexican view of the North American free trade agreement. *Columbia Journal of World Business* 32 (Summer): 79-81.

Beamish, Paul W., J. Peter Killing, Donald J. LeCraw, and Harold Crookell. 1991. *International management--text and cases.* Homewood, IL: Richard D. Irwin, Inc.

Beardsley, J. 1988. The evolution of participative management: American business culture. *Journal for Quality and Participation* 11, 1 (March): 38-42.

Bennis, Warren G., and Edgar H. Schein, eds. 1966. *Leadership and motivation--essays of Douglas McGregor*. Cambridge, Mass: The M.I.T. Press.

Berry, J. W. 1979. Research in multicultural societies: Implications of cross-cultural methods. *Journal of Cross-Cultural Psychology* (December): 415-424.

Bhagat, R. S., and S. J. McQuaid. 1982. Role of subjective culture in organizations: A review and directions for future research. *Journal of Applied Psychology Monograph* 67 (5): 653-685.

Bird, Allan, and Roger Dunbar. 1991. Getting the job done over there: Improving expatriate productivity. *National Productivity Review* 10, 2 (Spring): 145-156.

Blake, Robert R., and Jane Srygley Mouton. 1964. *The new managerial grid*. Houston: Gulf Publishing.

Boyd, Harper W., Ralph Westfall, and Stanley F. Stasch. 1989. *Marketing research*. 7th ed. Homewood, IL: Richard D. Irwin, Inc.

Boyd, Joseph A. 1990. Manufacturing: Key to America's future. Business Forum 15, 3 (Summer): 6-24.

Boseman, F. G., and A. Phatak. 1978. Management practices of industrial enterprises in Mexico: A comparative study. *Management International Review* 18 (1): 43-48.

Bottger, Preston C., Ingrid H. Hallein, and Philip W. Yetton. 1985. A cross-national study of leadership: Participation as a function of problem structure and leaders power. *Journal of Management Studies* 22, 4: 358-368.

Boyacigiller, Nakiye A., and Nancy J. Adler. 1991. The parochial dinosaur: Organizational science in a global contest. *The Academy of Management Review* 16, 2 (April): 262-290.

Bradburn, Norman M. and Seymour Sudman. 1979. *Improving interview method and questionnaire design*. San Francisco: Jossey-Bass Publishers.

Brislin, Richard W., Kenneth Cushner, Craig Cherrie, and Mahealani Yong. 1986. *International interactions--A Practical guide* Newbury Park: Sage Publications.

Bronson, Lou. 1994. Cross-cultural organization development. Organization Development Journal 12, 1 (Spring): 55-63.

Bryan, Gonzalez Vargas, and Gonzalez Baz. 1993. Foreign investment in Mexico--yesterday, today and tomorrow. In U.S. Department of Commerce Conference Proceedings, Dallas, Texas (January): 1-24.

Burack, Elmer H., and Nicholas J. Mathys. 1980. *Human resource planning--a pragmatic approach to manpower staffing and development*. Lake Forest, IL: Brace-Park Press.

Bureau of National Affairs. 1991. Maquiladoras will increase under NAFTA, speakers at conference agree. *Regulation, Economics, and Law*. Washington, DC: Government Printing Office.

Burger, Philip C., and Robert Doktor. 1976. Cross-cultural analysis of the structure of self-perception attitudes among managers from India, Italy, West Germany and the Netherlands. *Management International Review* (3): 76.

Burns, Tom, and G. M. Stalker. 1961. *The management of innovation*. London: Tavistock.

Bushnell, P. Timothy. 1994. *Transformation of the American manufacturing paradigm*. New York & London: Garland Publishing, Inc.

Butler, Mark C., and Mary B.Teagarden. 1993. Strategic management of worker health, safety, and environmental issues in Mexico's maquiladora inustry. *Human Resource Management* 32, 4 (Winter): 479-503.

Byars, Lloyd L. 1991. *Strategic management-formulation and implementation*. 3d ed. New York: Harper Collins Publishers, Inc.

Byrne, John A., Kathleen Kerwin, Amy Cortese, and Paula Dwyer. 1994. Borderless management--Companies strive to become truly stateless. *Business Week* (23 May): 24-5.

Campbell, Donald T., and Julian C. Stanley. 1963. *Experimental and quasi-experimental designs for research.* Boston: Houghton Mifflin Company.

Campbell, Donald T., William Bommer, and Ellen Yeo. 1993. Perceptions of appropriate leadership style: Participation versus consultation across two cultures. *Asia Pacific Journal of Management* 10, 1 (April): 1-20.

Carlin, Claudia. 1994. Pioneering partnerships south of the border. *Mexico--Business and Life* 1, 2 (April/May): 24-26.

Champion, Dean J. 1981. *Basic statistics for social research.* 2d ed. New York: McMillan Publishing Co., Inc.

Chandler, Alfred D. 1962. *Strategy and structure: Chapters in the history of the American industrial enterprise.* Cambridge, Massachusetts: MIT Press.

Chandler, Alfred D. 1986. The evolution of modern global competition. In *Competition in global industries.* ed. M. E. Porter, 28-39. Boston, Mass: Harvard Business School Press.

Child, John D. 1981. Culture, contingency and capitalism in the cross-national study of organizations. In *Research in organizational behavior* ed. B. M. Staw and L. T. Cummings, 151-154. Greenwich, CT: JAI Press.

Chisholm, K. Ann. 1988. Bruce Springsteen and the rhetoric of transformation. Master's thesis. University of North Carolina.

Choate, Pat, and Juyne Linger. 1988. Tailored trade: Dealing with the world as it is. *Harvard Business Review* (January-February): 90.

Clinton signs NAFTA, urges countries to support GATT. 1993. *Corpus Christi Caller-Times* (9 December): A17.

Collins, Denis, Ruth Ann Ross, and Timothy L. Ross. 1989. Who wants participative management? The managerial perspective. *Group & Organizational Studies* 14, 4 (December): 422-445.

The complete twin plant guide--Volumes I, II, and III. 1991. El Paso, Texas: Solunet.

Conover, W. J. 1980. *Practical nonparametric statistics.* 2d ed. New York: John Wiley Sons.

Conover, W. J., and Ronald L. Iman. 1981. Rank transformations as a bridge between parametric and nonparametric statistics. *The American Statistician* 35, 3 (August): 29-43.

Conrad, Charles. 1990. *Strategic organizational communication.* Fort Worth: Holt, Rinehart, and Winston.

Corrigan, E. H., president of Corrigan Company, Customs Brokerage Firm and Freight Forwarders, Laredo, Texas. Interview by author, 1 March 1991. Speaker at Symposium on Helping International Business Help Texas.

Crosbie, John. 1991. North American competitiveness and the Canada-US free trade agreement. *Harvard International Review* 13, 43 (Summer): 9-11, 59.

Crouch, Andrew, and Philip Yetton. 1988. The management team: An equilibrium model of management performance and behavior. In *Emerging leadership vistas.* ed. James G. Hunt, et al., 98-120. Lexington, Mass: Lexington Books.

Cummings, Thomas G. 1978. Self-regulating work groups: A sociotechnical synthesis. *Academy of Management Review* 12 (July): 625-634.

Cypher, John. 1991. Trade pact has enormous potential for all three countries. *Corpus Christi Caller-Times*, 13 April, 19(A).

Czinkota, Michael R., Ilkka A. Ronkainen, and Michael H. Moffett. 1994. *International business*, 3d ed. Fort Worth: The Dryden Press.

Daft, Richard L. 1989. *Organization theory and design.* 3d ed. St. Paul: West Publishing Co.

____. 1993. *Organization theory and design.* 4th ed. St. Paul: West Publishing Co.

Daft, Richard L., and Arie Y. Lewin. 1993. Where are the theories for the 'new' organizational forms? An editorial essay. *Organization Science* 4, 4 (November): i-v.

Danforth, John (U.S. Senator), and Sander Levin (U.S. Representative). NAFTA debate televised on September 12, 1992. Evans and Novak Transcript #130.

Daniels, John D., and Lee H. Radebaugh. 1989. *International business--environments and operations*. 5th ed. Reading, Mass: Addison-Wesley Publishing Co.

David, Fred R. 1991. *Strategic management*. 3d ed. New York: Macmillan Publishing Co.

Davidson, William H., and Jose de la Torre. 1989. *Managing the global corporation-case studies in strategy and management*. New York: McGraw-Hill Publishing Co.

Davis, Herbert J., and S. Anvaar Rasool. 1988. Values research and managerial behavior: Implications for devising culturally consistent managerial styles. *Management International Review* 28 (3):11.

Davis, Keith. 1963. The case for participative management. *Business Horizons* 6 (June): 55-60.

_____. 1957. *Human relations in business*. New York: McGraw-Hill Book Company.

Davis, P. 1986. An analysis of industry forces, corporate strategy, and business strategy as factors explaining business unit performance. Ph.D. diss., University of South Carolina.

Davis, S. M. 1969. United States versus Latin America: Business and culture. *Harvard Business Review*. 6 (November-December): 10-18.

Deal, Terrence, and Allen A. Kennedy. 1982. *Corporate cultures-- the rites and rituals of corporate life*. Reading, Mass: Addison-Wesley Publishing Co., Inc.

De la Torre, Jose, and Brian Toyne. 1978. Cross-national managerial interaction: A conceptual model. *The Academy of Management Review* 3, 3 (July): 462-474.

Del Giudice, Vincent. 1994. U.S. trade deficit surges by 7.6%. *Houston Chronicle* 20 July: 1(B), 3(B).

De Meuse, Kenneth P., and S. Jay Liebowitz. 1981. An empirical analysis of team-building research. *Group Organization Studies* 6 (3): 357-378.

Deming, W. Edwards. 1982, 1986. *Out of the crisis*. Cambridge, Mass: Massachusetts Institute of Technology.

_____. 1987. Transformation of today's management. *Executive Excellence* 4, 12 (December): 8.

Dess, G., and P. Davis. 1984. Porter's generic strategies as determinants of strategic group membership and organizational performance. *Academy of Management Journal* 27 (December): 467-488.

Dian, Natalie. 1994. An intercultural approach to organizational intervention. *Organization Development Journal* 12, 1 (Spring): 29-32.

Dill, William R. 1958. Environment as an influence on managerial autonomy. *Administrative Science Quarterly* 8 (March): 409-443.

Dillman, Don A. 1978. *Mail and telephone surveys--the total design method.* New York: John Wiley & Sons.

Doktor, Robert, Rosalie L. Tung, and Mary Ann Von Glinow. 1991a. Incorporating international dimensions in management theory building. *The Academy of Management Review* 16, 2 (April): 259-261.

Dominguez, Jorge I. 1987. Revolution and Flexibility in Mexico. In *Ideology and national competitiveness--An analysis of nine countries,* ed. G. C. Lodge and E. F. Vogel, 339-352. Boston, Mass: Harvard Business School Press.

Dornbusch, Rudiger. 1991. North American free trade. *Columbia Journal of World Business* 32 (Summer): 73-76.

Downing, George D., and Victor Soria M. 1976. Management development in Mexico: A crucially needed resource. *Arizona Business* 11 (January): 3-10.

Doz, Y., and C. Prahalad. 1988. Quality of management: An emerging source of global competitive advantage. In *Strategies in global competition,* ed. N. Hood and J. Vahlne, 54-62. New York: Croom Helm.

Drucker, Peter F. 1990. Mexico's ugly duckling--The maquiladora. *The Wall Street* Journal 4 October, 18-22.

_____. 1992. Managing for the future. *San Antonio Light* 5 April: 1(K), 6(K).

_____. 1993. A turnaround primer. *The Wall Street Journal* 2 February, A10.

Dumaine, Brian. 1990. Who needs a boss?--Not employees in self-managed teams. *Fortune* 121, 10 (7 May): 52-60.

_____. 1993. Payoff from the new management. *Fortune* 128, 15 (13 December): 103-113.

Dumville, James. 1994. Downsizing a part of global economy. *Corpus Christi Caller-Times* 11 July, 1, 8(D).

Duran, Eduardo, Deputy Trade Commissioner of Mexico. 1993. Symposia presentation at Business Association of Latin America Studies (BALAS) conference, Los Angeles, California, March 25.

Dymsza, William A., and Anant R. Negandhi. 1983. Introduction to cross-cultural management issues. *Journal of International Business Studies* 14, 2 (Fall: 15-16.

Edstrom, Anders, and Peter Lorange. 1984. Matching strategy and human resources in multinational corporations. *Journal of International Business Studies* 14 (Fall): 15-137.

Emery, F. E., and E. L. Trist. 1973. The causal texture of organizational environments. In *Readings in managerial psychology*, 2d ed., ed. Harold J. Leavitt and Louis R. Pondy, 170-189. Chicago: The University of Chicago Press.

Emory, C. William. 1976. *Business research methods*. Homewood, IL: Richard D. Irwin, Inc.

England, George W. 1975a. *The manager and his values: An international perspective from the United States, Japan, Korea, India, and Australia*. Cambridge, Mass: Ballinger Publishing Company.

_____. 1975b. Research instrument: Personal values questionnaire. In G. W. England, *The manager and his values: An international perspective from the United States, Japan, Korea, India, and Australia*, 131-139. Cambridge, Mass: Ballinger Publishing Company.

England, George W., and Itzhak Harpaz. 1983. Some methodological and analytic considerations in cross-national comparative research. *Journal of International Business Studies* 14, 2 (Fall): 49-59.

England, George W., and R. Lee. 1979. The relationship between managerial values and managerial success in the United States, Japan, India, and Australia. *Journal of Applied Psychology* 59 (4): 411-419.

England, George W., A. R. Negandhi, and B. Wilpert. 1981. *Organizational functioning in a cross-cultural environment.* Kent, Ohio: Comparative Administrative Research Institute.

Ernst and Young and American Quality Foundation. 1991. *International Quality Study.* Published research findings. Chicago, IL: American Quality Foundation.

Estrada, Richard. 1991. The danger of stereotyping. *Corpus Christi-Caller Times.* 6 May, ll(A).

Evan, William M. 1975. Measuring the impact of culture on organizations. *International Studies of Management & Organization* 5 (1): 91-113.

Evans, W. A., D. Sculli, and W. S. L. Yau. 1987. Cross-cultural factors in the identification of managerial potential. *Journal of General Management* 13, 1 (Autumn): 52-59.

Everett, J. E., and B. W. Stening. 1983. Japanese and British managerial colleagues--how they view each other. *Journal of Management Studies* (October): 467-475.

Feldstein, Martin. 1994. Competing in the world economy: Trade competition vs. growth competition. *Business Economics* XXIX, 1 (January): 7-23.

Ferrari, Sergio. 1972. Human behavior in international groups. *Management International Review* 12 (6): 31-5.

____. 1977. A Mexican approach to industrial training. *Management Industrial Review* 17 (June): 4.

Fiedler, Fred E. 1967. *A theory of leadership effectiveness.* New York: McGraw-Hill Publishers.

Fiedler, Fred E., Martin M. Chemers, and Linda Mahar. 1976. *Improving leadership effectiveness--the leader match concept.* New York: John Wiley & Sons.

Fiedler, Fred E., T. Mitchell, and Harry C. Triandis. 1971. The culture assimilator: An approach to cross-cultural training. *Journal of Applied Psychology* 13 (April): 95-102.

Fiol, C. Marlene. 1991. Managing culture as a competitive resource: An identity-based view of sustainable competitive advantage. *Journal of Management* 17 191-211.

FIPSE Transculturation Program for Faculty. 1990-1992. (Grant from the U.S. Department of Education's Fund for the Improvement of Post Secondary Education). Texas A&M University-Kingsville.

Fisher, K. Kim. 1986. Management roles in the implementation of participative management systems. *Human Resource Management* 25, 3 (Fall): 459-479.

Fombrun, Charles J., and Stefan Wally. 1992. Global entanglements: The structure of corporate transnationalism. In *Globalizing management.* eds. V. Pucik, N. M. Tichy, and C. K. Barnett, 15-46. New York: John Wiley & Sons, Inc.

French, J. R. P., J. Israel, and D. As. 1960. An experiment on participation in a Norwegian factory. *Human Relations* 13 (November): 14-29.

Fuller, Stephen H. 1980. How to become the organization of the future. *Management Review* 69, 2 (February): 50-53.

Furnham, Adrian, Bruce D. Kirkcaldy, and Richard Lynn. 1994. National attitudes to competitiveness, money, and work among young people: First, second, and third world differences. *Human Relations* 47 (1): 119-132.

Furr, Steve. 1991. Perspectives for the maquiladora industry within the free trade agreement. In *Labor review,* 4th ed., 109-111. Dallas, TX: U.S. Department of Trade.

Galbraith, C., and D. Schendel. 1983. Empirical analysis of strategy types. *Strategic Management Journal* 4 (April): 153-173.

Garland, Don, and Richard M. Farmer. 1986. *International dimensions of business policy and strategy.* Boston: Kent Publishing Co.

General agreement on tariffs and trade (GATT). 1994. GATT Hotline, U.S. Department of Commerce, International Trade Administration (June): 1-32.

George, Jill, Marilyn Perkins, Eric Sundstrom, and Stephanie Myers. 1990. Work-team context, development, and effectiveness in a manufacturing organization: A longitudinal study. *Proceedings from the 1990 International Conference of Self-Managed Work Teams.* M. Beyerlein and C. Miller, eds. University of North Texas.

Glaser, Daniel A., and Rose E. Knotts. 1993. Self-managed work teams: What are their chances for success in Mexico? Unpublished conference paper from the Business Association of Latin American Studies (BALAS) conference, Los Angeles, California.

Goddard, Robert W. 1991. A new view of work. *Supervision* 52, 4 (April): 14-16, 26.

Gonzales, R. F., and C. McMillan, Jr. 1961. The universality of American management philosophy. The *Academy of Management Journal* 41 (May): 33-41.

Goodman, P. S., R. Devades, and T. L. Hughson. 1988. Groups and productivity: Analyzing the effectiveness of self-managing teams. In *Productivity in organizations.* ed. J. P. Campbell, and R. J. Campbell, 221-239. San Francisco, California: Jossey-Bass.

Gray, Jerry L., and Frederick A. Starke. 1984. *Organizational behavior--concepts and applications,* 3d ed. Columbus: Charles E. Merrill Publishing Company.

Griffeth, R. W., P. W. Hom, A. DeNii, and W. Kirchner. 1980. A multivariate multinational comparison of managerial attitudes. *Proceedings.* Academy of Management, Detroit, 63-67.

Guest, Charlotte. 1991. Work team concept reaches across nation. *The North Texan* 41 (3): 3.

Guest, Robert H. 1979. Quality of work life--Learning from Tarrytown. *Harvard Business Review* 19 (July-August): 16-25.

Gundry, Lisa, Charles W. Prather, and Jill R. Kickul. 1994. Building the creative organization. *Organizational Dynamics* (Spring): 22-36.

Hackman, J. Richard. 1986. The psychology of self-management in organizations. In *Psychology and work: Productivity change and employment*. ed. M. S. Pollack and R. O. Perloff, 101-119. Washington, DC: American Psychological Association.

Hackman, J. Richard, and Edward E. Lawler. 1971. Employee reactions to job characteristics. *Journal of Applied Psychology Monograph* 55 (January): 259-286.

Hackman, J. Richard, and Greg R. Oldham. 1980. *Work redesign*. Reading, Massachusetts: Wesley.

Haire, Mason, Edwin E., Ghiselli, and Lyman W. Porter. 1966. *Managerial thinking: An international study*. New York: Wiley and Sons.

Haire, Mason, Edwin E. Ghiselli, and Lyman W. Porter. 1969. Cultural patterns in the role of the manager. In *Culture and management*. ed. Ross A. Webber, 280-301. Illinois: Richard D. Irwin, Inc.

Hambrick, D. C. 1983. High profit strategies in mature capital goods industries: A contingency approach. *Academy of Management Journal* 26 (March): 687-707.

Hamilton, Nora, and Eun Mee Kim. 1993. Economic and political liberalisation in South Korea and Mexico. *Third World Quarterly* 14 (1): 109-136.

Hammer, Michael, and James Champy. 1993. *Reengineering the corporation*. New York: HarperBusiness.

Hanson, Niles. 1981. *The border economy--regional development in the southwest*. Austin, Texas: University of Texas Press.

Harris, Philip R., and Robert T. Moran. 1991. *Managing cultural differences*. 3d ed. Houston, Texas: Gulf Publishing Company.

Harrison, Ann E. 1994. Productivity, imperfect competition and trade reform: Theory and evidence. *Journal of International Economics* 36, 1/2 (February): 53-73.

Haslett, Beth. 1989. Communications and language acquisition with a cultural context. In *Language, communications, and culture.* ed. Ting-Toomey and Korzenny, 17-26. Newberry Park: Sage Publications.

Haviland, William A. 1987. Cultural anthropology, 5th ed. New York: Hold, Rinehart and Winston, Inc.

Hayes, John, and Christopher W. Allinson. 1988. Cultural differences in the learning styles of managers. *Management International Review*, 28 (3): 75-80.

Healey, Nigel M. 1992. Is the United States turning protestionist? *Business & the Contemporary World* IV, 3 (Summer): 24-29.

Heenan, David A. 1993. After Nafta: The long-term benefits. *Business Strategy* 14, 2 (March/April): 5-8.

Herbig, Paul A., and Cynthia McCarty. 1993. National management of innovation:Interactions of culture and structure. *Multinational Business Review* 1, 1 (Spring): 19-26.

Hershey, Paul, and K. H. Blanchard. 1969. *Management of organizational behavior.* Englewood Cliffs, NJ: Prentice-Hall.

Herzberg, Frederick, Bernard Mausner, and Barbara Bloch Shyderman. 1959. *The motivation to work,* 2d ed. New York: John Wiley & Sons, Inc.

Hill C. 1988. Differentiation versus low cost or differentiation and low cost: A contingency framework. *Academy of Management Review* 13 (October): 401-412.

Hodgetts, Richard M., and Fred Luthans. 1991. *International management.* New York: McGraw-Hill, Inc.

____. 1994. *International management,* 2d ed. New York: McGraw-Hill, Inc.

Hofstede, Geert. 1980a. *Cultures consequences: International differences in work-related values.* Beverly Hills, CA: Sage Publications.

____. 1980b. Questions from research instrument: Hermes attitude survey questionnaire. In G. Hofstede, *Cultures consequences: International differences in work-related values,* 403-410. Beverly Hills, CA: Sage Publications.

_____. 1980c. Motivation, leadership, and organization: Do American theories apply abroad? *Organizational Dynamics* 5 (Summer): 42-63.

_____. 1983a. The cultural relativity of organizational practices and theories. *Journal of International Business Studies* 14 (2): 75-89.

_____. 1983b. National cultures in four dimensions: A research-based theory of cultural differences among nations. *International Studies of Management and Organization* 22 (Spring-Summer): 46-74.

_____. 1984a. Cultural dimensions in management and planning. *Asia Pacific Journal of Management* 1 (2): 81-99 .

_____. 1984b. The cultural relativity of the quality of life concept. *Academy of Management Journal* 9 (3): 389-398.

_____. 1985. The interaction between national and organizational value systems. *Journal of Management Studies* 22 (4): 347-368.

_____. 1987. The applicability of McGregor's theories in Southeast Asia. *The Journal of Management Development* 6 (3): 9-18.

_____. 1991. *Cultures and organizations--Software of the mind.* London: McGraw-Hill Book Company.

_____. 1992. Cultural dimensions in people management: The socialization perspective. In *Globalizing management*. eds. V. Pucik, N. M. Tichy, and C. K. Barnett, 139-158. New York: John Wiley & Sons, Inc.

Hofstede, Geert, and Michael H. Bond. 1988. The confucius connection: From cultural roots to economic growth. *Organizational Dynamics* 13 (Spring): 4-21.

Holmes, Michael. 1991. Salinas addresses lawmakers--Mexican president sees free-trade plan as boon to both sides. *Corpus Christi Caller-Times*, 13 April, l(A), 20(A).

Hosmer, LaRue Tone. 1982. The importance of strategic leadership. *Journal of Business Strategy* 3 (December): 47-57.

House, Robert J. 1971. A path-goal theory of leader effectiveness. *The Administrative Science Quarterly* 16 (March): 321-338.

Huck, Schuyler W., William H. Cormier, and William G. Bounds, Jr. 1974. *Reading statistics and research.* New York: Harper & Row, Publishers.

Hufbauer, Gary Clyde, and Jeffrey J. Schott. 1993. *Nafta--an assessment,* revised ed. Washington, D.C.: Institute for International Economics.

Hunt, James G., B. Rajaram Baliga, H. Peter Dachler, and Chester A. Schriesheim, eds. 1988. *Emerging leadership vistas.* Lexington, Mass: D. C. Heath and Co.

Jaeger, Alfred M. 1986. Organizational development and national culture: Where's the fit? *The Academy of Management Review* 11, 1 (January): 178-189.

_____. 1983. The transfer of organizational culture overseas: An approach to control in the multinational corporation. Journal of International Business Studies 14, 2 (Fall): 91-114.

Jago, Authur G. 1982. Leadership: Perspectives in theory and research. *Management Science* 28, 3 (March): 315-336.

Jain, Subhash C. 1990. *International marketing management,* 3d ed. Boston: PWS-Kent Publishing Co.

Jelinek, Mariann, Linda Smircich, and Paul Hirsch. 1983. Introduction [organizational culture]: A coat of many colors. *Administrative Science Quarterly* 28 (3): 331-335.

Joynt, Pat, and Malcolm Warner. 1985. *Managing in different cultures.* Oslo Norway: Universitetsforlaget AS. Kachigan, Sam Kash. 1986. *Statistical analysis.* New York: Radius Press.

Kahn, William A., and Kathy E. Kram. 1994. Authority at work: Internal models and their organizational consequences. *The Academy of Management Review* 19, 1 (January): 17-50.

Kanin-Lovers, J. 1990. Meeting the challenge of workforce 2000. *Journal of Compensation & Benefits* 5 (4): 233-235.

Kanter, Rosabeth Moss. 1983. *The change masters.* New York: Simon & Schuster.

Kanter, Rosabeth Moss, David V. Summers, and Barry A. Stein. 1986. The future of workplace alternatives, *Management Review* 75, 7 (July): 30-33.

Kast, Fremont E., and James E. Rosenzweig. 1972. General systems theory: Applications for organization and management. *Academy of Management Journal* 10 (December): 447-477.

Kedia, Ben L., and Rabi S. Bhagat. 1988. Cultural constraints on transfer of technology across nations: Implications for research in international and comparative management. *Academy of Management Review* (October): 559-571.

Kelley, Lane, and Reginald Worthley. 1981. The role of culture in comparative management: A cross-cultural perspective. *Academy of Management Journal* 25 (August): 164-173.

Kelley, Lane, Arthur Whatley, and Reginald Worthley. 1987. Assessing the effects of culture on managerial attitudes: A three-culture test. *Journal of International Business Studies* 19 (Summer): 17-31.

Kerlinger, Fred N. 1973. *Foundations of behavioral research*. 2d ed. New York: Holt, Rinehard and Winston, Inc.

Khanna, Sri Ram. 1986. Asian companies and the country stereotype paradox: An empirical study. *Columbia Journal of World Business* (Summer): 29-38.

Kidder, Louise H., and Charles M. Judd. 1986. *Research methods in social relations*. New York: Holt, Rinehart and Winston.

Kim, W. Chan, and Renee A. Mauborgne. 1987. Cross-cultural strategies. *The Journal of Business Strategy* 7, 4 (Spring): 28-36.

Kim, W. Chan, and Renee A. Mauborgne. 1993. Making global strategies work. *Sloan Management Review* 34, 3 (Spring): 11-27.

Klein, Janice A. 1991. A reexamination of autonomy in light of new manufacturing practices. *Human Relations* 44 (1): 21-38.

Kleist, Trina. 1992. Investors seek riches in Mexico--companies south of the border are growing in popularity. *Corpus Christi Caller-Times*, 23 March, 8(C), 9(C).

Kluckholn, F., and F. Strodtbeck. 1961. *Variations in value orientations*. Evanston, IL: Row, Peterson.

Knotts, Rose. 1989. Cross-cultural management: Transformations and adaptations. *Business Horizons* 32, 1 (January-February): 29-33.

Kootnikoff, Lawrence. 1991. Coming together--Forging the world's largest free-trade zone. *Business Mexico* 1, 1 (March): 4-10, 36-43.

Kotter, John P. 1988. *The leadership factor.* New York: The Free Press.

Kreitner, Robert, and Angelo Kinicki. 1989. *Organizational behavior.* Boston, MA: Richard D. Irwin, Inc.

Krishnan, Rama. 1974. Democratic participation in decision making by employees in American corporations. *Academy of Management Journal* 17, 2 (June): 339-347.

Kusy, Mitchell E., Linda Isaacson, and Joe Podolan. 1994. Encouraging upward influence through employee involvement. *Organization Development Journal* 12, 1 (Spring): 47-53.

Kvanli, Alan H., C. Stephens Guynes, and Robert J. Pavur. 1986. *Introduction to business statistics--A computer integrated approach.* St. Paul: West Publishing Company.

Lammers, C. J., and D. J. Hickson, eds. 1979. *Organizations alike and unlike: International and inter-institutional studies in the sociology of organizations.* London: Routledge & Kegan Paul.

Lane, Henry W., and Joseph J. DiStefano. 1992. *International management behavior*, 2d ed. Boston: PWS-Kent.

Laurent, Andre. 1983. The cultural diversity of western conceptions of management. *International Studies of Management and Organizations* 13, 1-2: 75-96.

_____. 1992. The cross-cultural puzzle of global human resosurce management. In *Globalizing management.* eds. V. Pucik, N. M. Tichy, and C. K. Barnett, 174-186.

Laurent, H. 1970. Cross-cultural validation of empirically validated tests. *Journal of Applied Psychology* 54 (December): 417-423.

Lawler, Edward E., III. 1973. *Motivation in work-related organizations.* Monterey, CA: Brooks/Cole.

_____. 1978. The new plant revolution. *Organizational Dynamics* 6 (3): 2-12.

____. 1985. Education, management style, and organizational effectiveness. *Personnel Psychology* 38 (1): 1-26.

____. 1986. *High-involvement management.* San Francisco: Jossey-Bass Publishers.

____. 1990. The new plant revolution revisited. *Organizational Dynamics* 19, 2: 4-14.

Lawler, Edward E., III, D. A. Nadler, and C. Cammann. 1980. *Organizational Assessment.* New York: Wiley and Sons.

Leontiades, James. 1986. Going global--Global strategies vs national strategies. *Long Range Planning* 19 (December): 96-105.

Le Vine, R. A., and O. T. Campbell. 1972. *Ethnocentrism: Theories of conflict, attitudes, and group behavior.* London: Wiley and Sons.

Levy, Linda. 1991. Training for the new competitive standards. *Twin Plant News* 7, 3 (October): 59, 86.

Lewis, Jordan D. 1991. Competitive alliances redefine companies. *Management Review* (AMA) 32 (April): 14-18.

Likert, Jane Gibson, personal communication. 1984. The Likert legacy: System 5 and new organizational forms for the future. Boston: *Academy of Management.*

Likert, Rensis. 1961. *New Patterns of management.* New York: McGraw-Hill Book Company, Inc.

____. 1967. *The human organization: Its management and value.* New York: McGraw-Hill Book Company, Inc.

____. 1971. The principle of supportive relationships. In *Organization theory,* ed. D. S. Pugh, 12-25. England: Penguin Books, Ltd.

Likert, Rensis, and Jane Gibson Likert. 1976. *New ways of managing conflict.* New York: McGraw-Hill.

Lincoln, James R., Mitsuyo Hanada, and Jon Olson. 1981. Cultural orientations and individual reactions to organizations: A study of employees of Japanese-owned firms. *Administrative Science Quarterly* 26 (December): 93-115.

Lodge, George C. 1987. The United States: The costs of ambivalence. In *Ideology and national competitiveness-An analysis of nine countries.* eds. George C. Lodge and Ezra F. Vogel, 212-256. Boston, MA: Harvard Business School Press.

Lorsch, Jay W. 1987. Managing culture: The invisible barrier to strategic change. In *Readings in strategic management*, 2d ed. ed. A. A. Thompson, A. J. Strickland, and W. E. Fulmer, 86-99. Plano, TX: Business Publications, Inc.

Maccoby, Michael. 1981. *The leader--A new face for American management.* New York: Simon and Schuster.

Maddox, Robert C., and Douglas Short. 1988. The cultural integrator. *Business Horizons* 31 (November-December): 57-60.

Magnet, Myron. 1992. The truth about the American worker. *Fortune* 125, 9 (4 May): 48-65.

Manz, Charles C., and Henry P. Sims, Jr. 1987. Leading workers to lead themselves: The external leadership of self-managing work teams. *Administrative Science Quarterly* 32 (June): 10-128.

Maquila scoreboard. 1994. *Twin Plant News* (June): 41.

Margulies, Newton, and Stewart Black. 1987. Perspectives on the implementation of participative approaches. *Human Resource Management* 26, 3 (Fall): 385-412.

Marks, M. L., P. H. Mirvis, E. J. Hackett, and J. F. Grady. 1986. Employee participation in a quality circle program: Impact on quality of work life, productivity, and absenteeism. *Journal of Applied Psychology* 71 (June): 61-69.

Massie, Joseph L., and Jan Luytjes, eds. 1972. *Management in an international context.* New York: Harper & Row, Publishers.

Maslow, Abraham H. 1965. *Eupsychian management.* Homewood, IL: Richard D. Irwin, Publishers.

Masur, Sandra. 1991. The North American free trade agreement. *Columbia Journal of World Business* 32 (Summer): 99-103.

Maurice, Marc. 1979. For a study of the 'societal effect': Universality and specificity in organization research. In *Organizations alike and unlike: International and inter-institutional studies in the sociology of organizations*, edited by Cornelis J. Lammers and David J. Hickson, 109-130. London, England: Routledge & Kegan Paul Ltd.

Maurice, Marc, A. Sorge, and M. Warner. 1980-1981. Societal differences in organizing manufacturing units: A comparison of France, West Germany and Great Britain. *International Studies of Management and Organization* 14 (Winter): 31-41.

Mawhinney, Thomas C. 1985. OBM, SPC, and theory D: A brief introduction. *Journal of Organizational Behavior* 8, 1 (Spring/Summer): 89-05.

McCray, John P., and Juan J. Gonzalez. 1989. Increasing global competitiveness with U.S.-Mexico maquiladora operations. *SAM Advanced Management Journal* 54, 3 (Summer): 4-48.

McGregor, Caroline, and Warren G. Bennis, eds. 1967. *The professional manager--Douglas McGregor.* New York: McGraw-Hill Book Company.

McGregor, Douglas. 1971. Theory X and Theory Y. In *Organization theory*, ed. D. S. Pugh, 15-40. England: Penguin Books, Ltd.

Meindl, James R. 1990. On leadership: An alternative to the conventional wisdom. *Research in Organizational Behavior* 12 (June): 159-203.

Meindl, James R., and Sanford B. Ehrlich. 1987. The romance of leadership and the evaluation of organizational performance. *Academy of Management Journal* 30 (1): 91-109.

Meyer, Michael C., and William L. Sherman. 1987. *The course of Mexican history*, 3d ed. New York: Oxford University Press.

Mexico--Background notes. 1994. United States Department of States, Bureau of Public Affairs V (4): 1-7.

Mexico Chamber of Commerce. 1990. *Mexico's maquiladora in-bond industry* (handbook). Published by the American Chamber of Commerce of Mexico, a.c. Mexico: Economic and social information. *INEGI International Review* 1, 1, (September-December): 14-24.

Mexico 2000: A classical analysis of the Mexican economy and the case supply-side economic reform. 1990. Morristown, IJ: Polyeconomics, Inc.

Miller, Danny. 1987. Strategy making and structure: Analysis and implications for performance. *Academy of Management Journal* 30 (1): 7-32.

Miller, Danny. 1988. Relating Porter's business strategies to environment and structure: Analysis and performance implications. *Academy of Management Journal* 31 (2): 280-308.

Miller, Danny, and P. Friesen. 1978. Archetypes of strategy formulation. *Management Science* 24 (June): 921-933.

Miller, Katherine I., and Peter R. Monge. 1986. Participation, satisfaction, and productivity: A meta-analytic review. *Academy of Management Journal* 29 (4): 727-753.

Miller, Stephen W., and Simonetti, Jack L. 1974. Culture and management: Some conceptual considerations. *Management International Review* 11 (5): 87-100.

Mintzberg, Henry. 1979. *The structuring of organizations.* Englewood Cliffs, NJ: Prentice-Hall, Inc.

_____. 1987. Crafting strategy. *Harvard Business Review* 65, 4 (July-August): 66-75.

_____. 1989. *Mintzberg on management.* New York: The Free Press.

Mirvis, Philip H., and Edward E. Lawler, III. 1980. Measuring the financial impact of employee attitudes. In *The study of organizations*, eds. Katz, Kahn, and Adams, 102-127. San Francisco: Jossey-Bass Publishers.

Mitchell, R. E. 1969. Survey materials collected in developing countries: Sampling, measurement, and interviewing obstacles to intra- and international comparisons. In *Comparative management and marketing*, ed. J. Boddewyn, 33-42. Glenview, IL: Scott, Foresman & Co.

Mittlelstadt, Michelle. 1994. NAFTA boosts economy--All three countries see increases from pact. *Corpus Christi Caller-Times* (19 August): A15, A19.

Miyajima, R. 1986. Organization ideology of Japanese managers. *Management International Review* 26 (1): 73-76.

Moore, R. 1974. The cross-cultural study of organizational behavior. *Human Organization* 33 (June): 37-45.

Moran, Robert T. 1988. A formula for success in multicultural organizations. *International Management* 43 (December): 74.

Morris, Tom. 1991. Productive management in Mexican maquiladoras: A comparative study. Unpublished paper presented at the BALAS Conference. Boston, Massachusetts.

Morrison, Allen J. 1990. *Strategies in global industries-- how U.S. businesses compete.* New York: Quorum Books.

Morse, John J., and Jay W. Lorsch. 1973. Beyond Theory Y. In *Readings in managerial psychology*, 2d ed. eds. Harold J. Leavitt and Louis R., Pondy, 28-41. Chicago: University of Chicago Press.

Mosbacher, Robert A., Secretary of Commerce. 1991. Executive summary. Symposium Proceedings, *North American free trade: Public and private partnership.* Texas A&M University, November.

Murphy, Robert F. 1989. *Cultural and social anthropology.* 3d ed. Englewood Cliffs, NJ: Prentice Hall.

Negandhi, Anant R. 1983. Cross-cultural management research: Trends and future directions. *Journal of International Business Studies* 14, 2 (all): 17-28.

Negandhi, Anant R., and B. Estafen. 1965. A research model to determine the applicability of American management know-how in differing cultures and/or environments. *Academy of Management Journal* 5 (December): 309-318.

Negroponte, John D., Ambassador. 1991. Continuity and change in U.S.-Mexican relations. *Columbia Journal of World Business* 32 (Summer): 7-10.

New Nafta tactic emerges in D.C.--White house shifts emphasis to foreign policy. 1993. *Corpus Christi Caller-Times* (7 November): A1, A16.

Newman, William. 1972. Cultural assumptions underlying U.S. management concepts. In *Management in an international context*. ed. Joseph L. Masie and Jan Luytjes, 77-101. New York: Harper & Row, Publishers.

Nibbe, D., and R. M. Nibbe, ed. 1994. Monthly scoreboard. *Twin Plant News*. Periodical published and edited by D. Nibbe and R. M. Nibbe. El Paso, Texas.

North American free trade agreement--Overview. 1992. U.S. Department of Commerce, Office of the U.S. Trade Representative (August): 1-54.

Norton, Erle. 1993. Future factories--Small, flexible plants may play crucial role in U.S. manufacturing. *The Wall Street Journal* (13 January): 1-2(A).

Nulty, Peter. 1990. The sound of an old machine. *Fortune* 21 May, 67-72.

Oberg, W. 1963. Cross-cultural perspectives on management principles. *Academy of Management Journal* 6 (July): 129-143

Ojeda, Mario. 1983. The future of relations between Mexico and the United States. In *U.S.-Mexico relations--Economic and social aspects*, eds. C. W. Reynolds and Carlos Tello, 44-59. Stanford, CA: Stanford University Press.

Ohmae, Kenichi. 1985. *Triad power: The coming shape of global competition*. New York: The Free Press.

_____. 1989. Managing in the borderless World. *Harvard Business Review* 30 (May-June): 152-161.

_____. 1990. *The borderless world--power and strategy in the interlinked economy*. New York: Harper Business.

Ott, J. Steven. 1989. *The organizational culture perspective*. Pacific Grove, CA: Brooks/Cole Publishing Company.

Ozawa, Terutomo. 1992. Foreign direct investment and economic development. *Transnational Corporations* 1, 1 (February): 27-54.

Parnell, John A., and Ben L. Kedia. 1994. The cultural dimension of international competitive advantage. *Central Business Review* XIII, 1 (Winter): 12-20.

Parsons, Talcott. 1960. *Structure and process in modern societies*. Glencoe, IL: The Free Press.

Pascarella, Perry. 1984. *The new achievers*. New York: The Free Press.

Pasmore, William. A., C. Francis, J. Haldeman, and A. Shani. 1982. Sociotechnical systems: A North American reflection on empirical studies of the seventies. *Human Relations* 35 (1): 1179-1204.

Pearce, John A., E. C. Ravlin. 1987. The design and activation of self-regulated work groups. *Human Relations* 40, 2: 751-782.

Pearce, John A., and Kendall Roth. 1988. Multinationalization of the mission statement. *Advancement Management Journal* 53 (Summer): 39-45.

Peters, Tom. 1988. *Thriving on chaos--handbook for a management revolution*. New York: Alfred A. Knopf.

Pfeffer, J. 1981. Management as symbolic action: The creation and maintenance of organizational paradigms. In *Research in organizational behavior* 3, eds. L. L. Cummings and B. M. Staw, 105-119. Greenwich, CT: JPI Press.

Phatak, Arvind V. 1989. *International dimensions of management*, 2d ed. Boston, MA: PWS-Kent Publishing Company.

Philip, George. 1993. The new economic liberalism and democracy in Latin America: Friends or enemies? *The Third World Quarterly* 14 (3): 555-572.

Podsakoff, Philip. M., Peter M. Dorfman, John P. Howell, and William D. Todor. 1986. Leader reward and punishment behaviors: A preliminary test of culture-free style of leadership effectiveness. *Advances in International Comparative Management* 2 (April): 95-138.

Polley, R. B. 1988. Intervention and cultural context: Mediation in the U.S. and Norway. Journal of Management 14 (4): 617-629.

Porter, Michael E. 1980. *Competitive strategy--techniques for analyzing industries and competitors*. New York: The Free Press.

_____. 1985. *Competitive advantage--creating and sustaining superior performance*. New York: The Free Press.

_____. 1990. *The competitive advantage of nations*. New York: The Free Press.

_____. 1991. Competitive advantage and global trade in the 1990s. *Harvard International Review* 13, 4 (Summer): 12-14, 59.

Porter, Roger B. 1992. United States investment policy. *Business & the Contemporary World* IV, 3 (Summer): 17-23.

Posner, Barry A., James M. Kouzes, and Warren H. Schmidt. 1985. Shared values make a difference: An empirical test of corporate culture. Human Resource Management 24, 3 (Fall): 293-309.

Preston, Lee E., and James E. Post. 1974. The third managerial revolution. *Academy of Management Journal* 17, 3 (September): 476-486.

Pucik, Vladimir. 1992. Globalization and human resource management. In *Globalizing management*. eds. V. Pucik, N. M. Tichy, and C. K. Barnett, 61-80. New York: John Wiley & Sons, Inc.

Pugh, Derek S., and David J. Hickson. 1989. *Writers on organizations*, 4th ed. Newbury Park, CA: Sage Publications, Inc.

Quinn, Robert P., and William Cobb, Jr. 1980. What workers want: Factor analyses of important ratings of job facets. In *The study of organizations*, eds. D. Katz, R. L. Kahn, and J. S. Adams, 225-251. San Francisco: Jossey-Bass Publishers.

Quintana, Fred. 1991. Maquilas, labor unions, and free trade. *Mexico Maquiladora--In-Bond Industry* (IV): 66-77.

Redding, S. G. 1980. Cognition as an aspect of culture and its relation to management processes: An exploratory view of the Chinese case. *Journal of Management Studies* 12 (May): 127-148.

Reynolds, Clark W., and Carlos Tello, eds. 1983. *U.S.-Mexico relationships--Economic and social aspects*. Stanford, CA: Stanford University Press.

Reudi, A., and Paul R. Lawrence. 1970. Organizations in two cultures. In *Studies in organization design*, ed. J. W. Lorsch and P. R. Lawrence, 334-365. Homewood, IL: Richard D. Irwin.

Rhinesmith, Stephen H. 1979. *Cultural-organizational analysis: The interrelationship of value orientations and managerial behavior*, Monograph. Pittsburgh: University of Pittsburgh.

Ricks, David A., Brian Toyne, and Zaida Martinez. 1990. Recent development in international management research. Yearly Review of Management. Special issue of *The Journal of Management* 16 (2): 219-253.

Robbins, Stephen P. 1988. *Management--concepts and applications*, 2d ed. Englewood Cliffs, NJ: Prentice-Hall.

Roberts, K. H. 1977. On looking at an elephant: An evaluaton of cross-cultural research related to organizations. In *Culture and management*, ed. P. D. Weishall, 53-71. New York: Penguin.

Robinson R., and J. Pearce. 1985. The structure of generic strategies and their impact on business-unit performance. *Academy of Management Proceedings*. San Diego, CA, 35-39.

Ronen, Simcha, and Allen I. Kraut. 1977. Similarities among countries based on employee work values and attitudes. *Columbia Journal of World Business* 32 (Summer): 89-96.

Ronen, Simcha, and Allen I. Kraut. 1985. Clustering countries on attitudinal dimensions: A review and synthesis. *Academy of Management Review* 10 (3): 435-454.

Rose, Frank. 1990. A new age for business? *Fortune* 8 October, 156-164.

Rugman, Alan M., and Michael Gestrin. 1993. The strategic response of multinational enterprises to Nafta. *Columbia Journal of World Business* XXVIII, IV (Winter): 18-29.

Sanderson, Susan W., and Robert H. Hayes. 1990. Mexico--Opening ahead of Eastern Europe. *Harvard Business Review* 28 (September-October): 32-41.

Sashkin, Marshall. 1986. Participative management remains an ethical imperative. *Organizational Dynamics* 14, 4 (Spring): 62-75.

Schein, Edgar H. 1986. *Organizational culture and leadership*. San Francisco: Jossey-Bass Publishers.

Schendel, Dan E., and Charles W. Hofer, eds. 1979. *Strategic management--a new view of business policy and planning*. Boston: Little, Brown and Company

Schermerhorn, John R., Jr., James G. Hunt, and Richard N. Osborn. 1985. *Managing organizational behavior*, 2d ed. New York: John Wiley & Sons.

Schneider, Susan C. 1988. National vs. corporate culture: mplications for human resource management. *Human Resource Management* 27, 2 (Summer): 231-246.

Schneider, Susan C., and Arnoud de Meyer. 1991. Interpreting and responding to strategic issues: The impact of national culture. *Strategic Management Journal* 12 (March): 307-320.

Schuler, Randall S., Peter J. Dowling, and Helen De Cieri. 1993. An integrative framework of strategic international human resource management. *Journal of Management* 19, 2 (Summer): 419-460.

Schwartz, Peter, and Jerry Saville. 1986. Multinational business in the 1990s--A scenario. Long Range Planning 19 (December): 31-38.

Schwebel, Gerald, Senior Vice-President of International Bank of Commerce, Laredo, Texas. 1991. Symposium on helping international business help Texas. Reprint of speech entitled border economic development and the strategic importance of Laredo. 2 March. Laredo, Texas.

Sekaran, Uma. 1981. Are U.S. organizational concepts and measures transferable to another culture? An empirical investigation. *Academy of Management Journal* 26 (June): 409-417.

_____. 1981. Nomological networks and the understanding of organizations in different cultures. Forty-First *Academy of Management Proceedings*, pp. 54-58. San Francisco, CA.

_____. 1983. Methodological and theoretical issues and advancements in cross-cultural research. *Journal of International Business Studies* 14, 2 (Fall): 61-73.

Sekarna, Uma, and H. J. Martin. 1982. An examination of the psychometric properties of some commonly researched individual differences, job, and organizational variables in other cultures. *Journal of International Business Studies* 14 (Spring/Summer): 51-66.

Serwer, Andrew E. 1994. Lessons from America's fastest-growing companies. *Fortune* 130, 3 (8 August): 42-62.

Shane, Scott. 1993. Cultural influences on national rates of innovation. *Journal of Business Venturing* 8, 1 (January): 59-74.

Sherwood, Robert. 1991. Personal Interview by author, 1 March, Plant Manager of Delredo subsidiary of General Motors. Nuevo Leon, Mexico.

Shrivastava, Paul, and Sidney A. Nachman. 1989. Strategic leadership patterns. *Strategic Management Journal* 10 (February): 51-66.

Siegel, Sidney. 1956. *Nonparametric statistics for the behavioral sciences*. New York: McGraw-Hill Book Company.

Slater, Stanley F. 1989. The influence of managerial style on business unit performance. *Journal of Management* 14 (3): 441-455.

Smircich, L. 1983. Concepts of culture in organizational analysis. *Administrative Science Quarterly* 28 (November): 339-358.

Smith, P. B., M. Tayeb, M. Peterson, M. Bond, and J. Misumi. 1990. On the generality of leadership style measures. Unpublished manuscript (1985) cited in B. M. Bass, *Bass & Stogdill's handbook of leadership--theory, research and managerial applications*, 3d ed., 551-579. New York: The Free Press.

Snodgrass, Coral R., and Edward J. Szewczak. 1991. Validation of a model to support the decision to transfer management control systems. *European Journal of Operational Research* 50, 2 (25 January): 157-165.

Special report: U.S. companies doing business in Mexico. *The Corporate Growth Report* 9, 8 (August): 10-11.

Stanford, Jane H. 1990. An analysis of questionnaire design: Opinion survey methodology. *Decision Sciences Theory and Applications Proceedings*. Twenty-First Annual Conference, Southwest Region, pp. 126-130.

Steel, Robert P., and Russell F. Lloyd. 1988. Cognitive, affective, and behavioral outcomes of participation in quality circles: Conceptual and empirical findings. *The Journal of Applied Behavioral Science* 24 (1): 1-17.

Stepanek, Marcia. 1994. Clinton hopes to reassure world leaders. *Corpus Christi Caller-Times* 3 July: A18.

Stevens, Dennis, and Paul Beamish. 1993. Global business--forging alliances in Mexico. *Business Quarterly* 58, 2 (Winter): 79-84.

Stewart, Edward C. 1972. *American cultural patterns: A cross-cultural perspective.* Chicago, IL: Intercultural Press, Inc.

Stewart, Thomas A. 1991. GE keeps those ideas coming. *Fortune*, 12 August, 40-49.

_____. 1992. The search for the organization of tomorrow. *Fortune*, 18 May, 92-98.

_____. 1993. Reengineering: The hot new managing tool. *Fortune*, 23 August, 40-48.

Stoner, James A. F., and R. Edward Freeman. 1992. *Management.* Englewood Cliffs, NJ: Prentice all.

Sunstrom, Eric, Kenneth P. De Meuse, and David Futrell. 1990. Work teams--applications and effectiveness. *American Psychologist* 45, 2 (February): 120-130.

Szekely, Gabriel and Oscar Vera. 1991. What Mexico brings to the table. *Columbia Journal of World Business* 32 (Summer): 29-36.

Tannenbaum, A. S. 1980. Organizational psychology. In *Handbook of cross-cultural psychology*, eds. Triandis and Brislin, 107-129. Boston: Allyn and Bacon.

Taola, George M., and Don R. Beeman. 1991. *International business--environments, institutions, and operations.* New York: Harper Collins, Publishers.

Terpstra, Vern, and Kenneth David. 1985. *The cultural environment of international business*, 2d ed. Cincinnati: Southwestern Publishing Co.

Thiederman, Sondra. 1988. Keys to effective cross-cultural motivation. *Manage* 40, 3 (October): 26.29.

Thomas, Alan B. 1988. Does leadership make a difference to organizational performance? *Administrative Science Quarterly* 33 (3): 388-399.

Thompson, Arthur A., Jr., and A. J. Strickland. 1992. *Strategic management--concepts and cases*, 6th ed. Boston, MA: Richard D. Irwin, Inc.

____. 1993. *Strategic management--concepts and cases*, 7th ed. Boston, MA: Richard D. Irwin, Inc.

Thorup, Cathryn L. 1991. The politics of free trade and the dynamics of cross-border coalitions in U.S.-Mexican relations. *Columbia Journal of World Business* 32 (Summer): 12-24.

Thurow, Lester. 1992. *Head to head--The coming economic battle among Japan, Europe, and America*. New York: William Morrow and Company, Inc.

Tichy, Noel M., Michael I. Brimm, Ram Charan, and Hiroraka Takeuchi. 1992. Leadership development as a lever for global transformation. In *Globabilizing management*. eds. V. Pucik, N. M. Tichy, and C. K. Barnett, 47-60. New York: John Wiley & Sons, Inc.

Torbiorn, Ingemar. 1985. The structure of managerial roles in cross-cultural settings. *International Studies of Management and Organizations* 15 (1): 52-74.

Triandis, Harry C. 1983. Dimensions of cultural variation as parameters of organizational theories. *International Studies of Management and Organizations* 14 (Winter): 139-169.

Triandis, Harry C., and Walter Lonner, eds. 1980. *Handbook of cross-cultural psychology*. Boston, MA: Allyn and Bacon, Inc.

Triandis, Harry C., V. Vassiliou, G. Vassiliou, Y. Tanaka, and A. Shanmugan. 1972. *The analysis of subjective culture*. New York: John Wiley and Sons.

Trist, E., and K. Bamforth. 1951. Social and psychological consequences of the long-wall method of coal getting. *Human Relations* 7 (February): 3-28.

Tung, Rosalie L. 1993. Managing cross-national and intranational diversity. *Human Resource Management* 32, 4 (Winter): 461-477.

Uchitelle, Louis. 1994. Overseas investments rising rapidly. *Corpus Christi Caller-Times* 31 July, 13-14(J).

U.S. seeks end to maquiladora barriers. *Corpus Christi Caller-Times* 19 May, 7(C).

Uruguay round: Jobs for the United States, growth for the world. 1993. Uruguay Round Hotline, U.S. Department of Commerce, International Trade Administration (December): 2-14.

Urwick, Lyndall F. 1970. Theory Z. *SAM Advanced Management Journal* 35 (January): 14-21.

Van, Jon. 1992. Business retools its way of thinking. *San Antonio Light* 16 February, 1-2(E).

Van Ark, Bart, and Dirk Pilat.1993. Productivity levels in Germany, Japan, and the United States: Differences and causes. In *Brookings papers on economic activity* (Brookings Panel on Microeconomics conference papers), eds. Martin Neil Baily, Peter C. Reiss, and Clifford Winston, 1-69. Washington, D.C.: Brookings Institution.

Van Fleet, David D. 1991. *Behavior in organizations*. Boston: Houghton Mifflin Company.

Vander Zanden, James W. 1965. *Sociology--A systematic approach*. New York: The Ronald Press Company.

Von Bertalanffy, L. 1950. The theory of open systems in physics and biology. *Science* 13 January, 23-29.

Vroom, Victor H. 1964. *Work and motivation*. New York: John Wiley & Sons, Inc.

Vroom, Victor H., and Phillip Yetton. 1973. *Leadership and decision making*. Pittsburgh: University of Pittsburgh Press.

Wallace, Roger W., Deputy under Secretary of International Trade. 1991. North American free trade agreement: Generating jobs for America. Symposium proceedings, North American Free Trade: Public and Private partnership. Texas A&M University, November.

Waller, Andrew. 1994. Winds of change--The GATT world-trade accord holds huge promise for Asia. *Far Eastern Economic Review* (28 April): 64-66.

Walsh, J. P. 1988. Selectivity and selective perception: An investigation of managers' belief structures and information processing. Academy of Management Journal 31 (June): 873-896.

Walton, Mary. 1986. *The Deming management method.* New York: Putnam Publishing Company.

Wartzman, Rick. 1992. Sharing gains--a whirlpool factory raises productivity--and pay of workers. *The Wall Street Journal* 89, 87, 4 May, 1(A) and 4(A).

Webber, Ross A. 1969. Convergence or divergence? *Columbia Journal of World Business* 4 (3): 75-83.

Webber, Ross A. 1969. *Culture and management.* Homewood, IL: Irwin Publishing Co.

Weisbord, Marvin R. 1988. For more productive workplaces. *Journal of Management Consulting* 4 (2): 7-14.

Wheelen, Thomas L., and J. David Hunger. 1990. *Strategic management,* 3d ed. Reading, MA: Addison-Wesley Publishing Company.

Wheelwright, Steven C. 1984. Manufacturing strategy: Defining the missing link. *Strategic Management Journal* 5 (September): 77-91.

Whetton, David A., and Kim S. Cameron. 1991. *Developing management skills,* 2d ed. New York: Harper Collins Publishers Inc.

Whip, Richard, Robert Rosenfeld, and Andrew Pettigrew. 1989. Culture and competitiveness: Evidence from two mature UK industries. *Journal of Management Studies* 26, 6 (November): 561-585.

Whiting, J. W. M. 1968. Methods and problems in cross-cultural research. In *The handbook of social psychology,* ed. G. Lindey and E. Aronson, 199-225. Reading, MA: Addison-Wesley.

Wittenberg-Cox, Avivah. 1991. Delivering global leaders. *International Management.* (Europe Edition) 46, 1 (February): 52-55.

Wren, Daniel A. 1987. *The evolution of management thought,* 3d ed. New York: John Wiley and Sons.

Wu, Terry, and Neil Longley. 1991. The U.S.-Canada free trade agreement. *Columbia Journal of World Business* 32 (Summer): 61-71.

Yeh, Rhy-song. 1988. Values of American, Japanese and Taiwanese managers in Taiwan: A test of Hofstede's framework. *Proceedings of the Academy of Management National Meeting.* Anaheim, CA.

Zeffane, Rachid. 1988. Participative management in centrally planned economies: Algeria and Yugoslavia. *Organization Studies* 9 (3): 393-422.

Glossary

GLOSSARY

Assembly Plant: Refers to the *maquiladora* or "twin" plants which are divided into main manufacturing headquarters on the United States side of the Mexico-U.S. border and assembly plant subsidiaries located on the Mexican side. Component parts are manufactured in the United States by a United States workforce, shipped to a subsidiary in Mexico, and assembled by a Mexican workforce that is typically managed by a United States expatriate. (See also "Maquiladora," "Twin Plants," and "In-Bond Assembly Industry").

Authoritative Management: An analogous term for this style of management is "top-down" management, which implies that policies and procedures are passed down through the hierarchical levels of management to employees. With this style of management, employees usually have little or no input into organizational decision making. Thus, this style is antithetical to participative or employee involvement. (See also "participative" and "employee involvement").

Corporate Culture versus National Culture: Corporate culture is the society that exists within an organization, while a national culture is the larger society to which an organization belongs.

Direct Foreign Investment (DFI): The flow of investment from one country to another, which can mean a controlling interest in a firm by foreign investors or can mean a wholly-owned business in a country owned by foreign investors. Most countries have laws governing the amount of direct investment that can be made by foreign investors. For example, since the passage of the North American Free Trade agreement (NAFTA), Mexico has relaxed its DFI policies for its two trading partners--Canada and the U.S.; however, NAFTA does accord Mexico the right to continue to screen foreign acquisitions above an initial threshold of $25 million. This figure will be progressively increased to $150 million (plus inflation adjustments) over 10 years beginning January 1, 1994. (See North American Free Trade Agreement).

Employee Involvement (EI): Refers to the contemporary terminology typically used in lieu of the term "participative management." EI is a management strategy or "style" that endeavors to involve employees at every level of the organization in decision making. This type of management is usually analogous to a "flat" organization versus a "tall," hierarchial or bureaucratic organization distinguished by centralized management. The flat organization has few levels of management because decision making is widespread among employees at all levels of the structure; i.e., the flat organization is characterized by decentralized management. (See also "participative management" and "authoritative management").

Expatriate Managers: Persons employed by a multinational organization who are citizens of the country where the MNC is based, but who work in one of the company's foreign operations. In this particular study, the reference to expatriate managers was to those individuals who are citizens of the United States but have managerial responsibilities in Mexican *maquiladora* subsidiaries of United States companies.

External Environment: This refers to an organization's constituencies that are external to the organization. These constituencies directly affect the organization or have the potential to do so, such as the societal culture, the national economy (and global economy in the case of an MNC), government policies and regulations, and competitors.

General Agreement on Tariffs and Trade (GATT): On December 15, 1993, 117 countries concluded a major agreement, initiated in 1986 in Punta del Este, Uruguay, to reduce barriers blocking exports to world markets, to extend coverage and enhance disciplines on critical areas of trade, and to create a more fair, more comprehensive, more effective, and more enforceable set of world trade rules. (Currently, 123 countries are involved in the pact, which has a January 1, 1995 ratification deadline). (See also Uruguay Round).

Home Country National Managers: Persons employed by a multinational organization who are citizens of the country where the MNC is based, and who work in a domestic facility. In this particular study, the reference to home country national managers was to those individuals who are citizens of the United States and work in the United States.

Host Country Workforce: Persons who are citizens of the country where the MNC has foreign operations. In this particular study, the reference to a host country workforce is to Mexican citizens working in the Mexico-based *maquiladora* plant facilities of a United States MNC.

In-Bond Assembly Industry: This term is used synonymously with "*maquiladora* industry" and referred to the practice of placing a "bond" on parts manufactured in the United States being transported into Mexico for assembly. When the completed goods were exported back to the U.S., the bond was lifted and a tariff was paid only on the "value-added" in Mexico. Originally the bond was a "guarantee" that the goods would not be sold in Mexico; e.g., a 1983 law placed a 20 percent ceiling on the amount of goods that could be sold in Mexico. With the growth of trade between the U.S. and Mexico and the passage of the North America Free Trade Agreement, the ceiling on *maquiladora* assemblied goods that can be sold in Mexico has been increasingly raised.

Maquiladora Industry or Program: Refers to the plan initiated by the Mexican government to bring labor-intensive industry into Mexico to use its large labor pool in order to ameliorate the country's high rate of unemployment. In this study, all references to this industry are only to the reciprocal agreement established between Mexico and the United States in 1965. (See also "In-Bond Assembly Industry," "Twin Plants," and "Assembly Plants").

Multinational (MNC) Organization: Companies based in one country that have a substantial direct investment in a foreign country and actively manage those operations and regard those operations as integral parts of the company, both strategically and organizationally.

National Culture versus Corporate Culture: National culture or societal culture is the larger society of which an organization is but a part; thus, corporate culture is the culture within an organization.

North American Free Trade Agreement (NAFTA): On December 17, 1992, the United States, Mexico, and Canada signed this historic trade accord. NAFTA is the most comprehensive free trade pact (short of a common market) ever negotiated between regional trading partners, and the first reciprocal free trade pact between a developing country and industrial countries. After being ratified by the three legislatures, NAFTA was implemented on January 1, 1994.

Participative Management: This term refers to the active involvement of employees in the decision making processes within an organization. A participative style of management is sometimes referred to as "bottom-up management" and is considered to be the opposite of "top-down" or authoritative management. In this study, the term "participative" connotes the *System 4* style of management advocated by Rensis Likert and other organizational theorists with similar managerial philosophies. Throughout this book, the term "participative" is used synonymously with employee involvement or "EI." (See also "employee involvement" and "authoritative management").

Systems 1, 2, 3, and 4: These terms were coined by Rensis Likert to denote particular styles of management. *Sytem 1* labeled a highly authoritative, exploitative style. *System 2* was moderately authoritative. *System 3* and *4* were participative styles; however, *System 3* was not as highly participative as was *System 4*.

Transferability Issue: This refers to the hypothesis posed by some international management theorists that management theory is "culture bound" to its country of origin and, therefore, cannot be readily and effectively implemented in or "transferred to" to a foreign setting by expatriates managing a host country workforce.

Twin Plants: This term refers to the particular configuration of the Mexico-U.S. *maquiladora* industry. In this dichotomous arrangement of company headquarters and plants, manufacturing facilities are headquartered in the U.S., while assembly plants or facilities are located in Mexico. (See also "*Maquiladora* Industry," "In-Bond Assembly Industry," and "Assembly Plants").

Uruguay Round: The talks that culminated in the current version of the General Agreement on Tariffs and Trade were launched in Punta del Este, Uruguay, in 1986; thus, the talks are usually referred to as the Uruguay Round. They were the latest and most significant set of negotiations that have been carried out periodically since the 1940s; i.e., following World War II, the major economic powers of the world, recognizing that obstacles to trade hindered economic development and growth, negotiated a set of rules for reducing and limiting barriers to trade and for settling trade disputes. These rules were called the General Agreement on Tariffs and Trade (GATT). (See also General Agreement on Tariffs and Trade).

General Index

General Index